# Do It Again!

## Wisdom for the Way of Marital Relationships and Personal Development

For permission requests, write to the publisher at:

Odyssey Media Group & Publishing
P.O. Box 681046
Houston, TX 77268

Printed in the United States of America
First Printing 2022

Berger, Jacquelyn, 1973 Berger, Tierre, 1969 — Author
Do It Again

This book has been written to share the concept of failure and what it means since most of us are misinformed about what it is. This book will challenge how you think. It is designed to be short and quick while offering valuable information. It will leave lasting impressions and ideas to motivate you.

People need a type of motivation that helps them through failure and setbacks in life, and often, they need it in a hurry. The fastest way of "Doing it Again" is to start this journey right where you are.

Like most people, we quickly want to give up when we mess up. We tend to cave in and quit. We may feel like we're at the bottom in our relationships - be it marriage, friendships, or both.

Rest assured, You are at the right place at the right time with this book!

# Table of Content

# Foreword

As a global life strategist, one of the most common "fallible paradigm parameters" is the concept that failure isn't an option. It sounds good when you say it; however, an unfulfilled state of mind sets you up for failure. Failure is a part of the growth process. I teach my clients that the goal is to fail forward—temporarily falling short of an inevitable reality, and that ultimate failure only comes through quitting. The concept of failing forward is visibly evident when it comes to marriage. While no one wants the word "failure" associated with their marriage, the truth is that we all fail as a part of the growth process.

**Tierre and Jacquelyn Berger** take significant yet measurable steps to outline the power of embracing failure as a part of the success equation. The idea of embracing failure is not to aspire to it but to understand how it works in our relationships and other endeavors. One thing that sets these two apart from so many self-proclaimed life coaches is their genuineness and inexorable passion for changing the lives of their clients. They are not simply spewing over-cycled rhetoric; they are sharing the principles that have allowed their marriage to thrive despite the inevitable challenges they have faced.

My experience has revealed that one of the most consistent obstacles people face when attempting to make significant changes is the fear of failure. Tierre and Jacquelyn provide critical insight into the need to understand how to process and frame their failures to remove the negative connotation and cognitive impact of failing. Having known and worked with Tierre for over a decade, I am keenly cognizant of his passion and intent. It comes out in his direct engagement with subjects and reveals itself in the truths outlined in this well-written guide to self-fulfillment in marriage and beyond, despite failures instead of their absence.

Jacquelyn brings the power of a well-honed spiritual intuition coupled with transcendent knowledge to the table. The term power couple is hyper-applied in today's culture; however, it is an understatement when describing Tierre and Jacquelyn Berger. Tierre clarifies that Jacquelyn isn't just some supplemental component but an integral element in compiling a resourceful guide to unmatched success in marriage and beyond.

I often say that there is no circumvention of the vicissitudes of life and the challenges that will come rolling into your paradise. I also teach that everything worth having in this life will be achieved through the painful process of overcoming initial failures. Tierre and Jacquelyn solidify this perspective in a highly skillful presentation throughout this book. No matter how caught up in fear of the idea of failing you have been, prepare to experience a massive change as the one thing you once feared becomes the catalyst for your elevation and success in your marriage and beyond.

~ Rick Wallace, Ph.D., Psy.D.
Global Life Strategist
Founder & CEO of The Visionetics Institute

# Acknowledgments

Thankful to be under the Power of The Most High's grace, mercy, and truth.

Jude 1:24-25

[24] Now unto him, that is able to keep you from falling, and to present you faultless before the presence of his glory with exceeding joy,

[25] To the only wise God our Savior, be glory and majesty, dominion and power, both now and ever. Amen

First, we want to thank the powers of heaven: the Father, the Son, and the Holy Spirit. For it was The Most High God, "Ahayah" (אהיה), the great "I Am" (Phoenician Hebrew). The name that he revealed to Moses in (Exodus 3:1-15, Leviticus 26:46, Joshua 24:17, and Exodus 20:2.

I am so incredibly grateful to the true and living God" Ahayah" for sending His dear son, our Savior, "Yashaya Christ" (ישעי), whom the world calls Jesus Christ, for giving us the idea to write this book and providing the method, materials, and means to make this all possible.

**From Coach Tierre**

I'm eternally grateful to a few key people. First and foremost, my wife, and my love: Coach Jacquelyn E. Berger, for working alongside me on this project with her research and exceptional input. I still don't know how I got so blessed to have such a wonderful, smart, and intelligent woman after all these years. Here we are, twenty-nine years later, and it still feels like yesterday that we first met at Long Branch Park in Killeen, TX.

I also want to thank our huge supporters, my mom, Elizabeth, and the late Mr. Paul L. Berger Jr. (R.I.P) for all their love and belief in my many projects, whether they understood them or not (smile). There are so many individuals we could name, especially all five of our grown children and grand baby. The names are too vast to call out individually, so I'll keep it simple; You know now who you are. I attribute and dedicate most of this book to the many conversations and memories of two of the greatest people in my life, my mom and dad.

**From Coach Jacquelyn**

I would also like to thank my mother, the great Betty J., and my father, the late Louis A. Pleasant. Mom, thank you for raising and teaching me to respect myself first and then others. Thank you for showing me how to love my children, my husband, and to always fear (have the utmost respect for) The Most High God. Dad (R.I.P) Thank you for loving me and raising me. Thank you for letting me be your "Bird" (nickname). I love you, daddy, for all the wonderful things that you showed me in my life. You taught me not to never take any wooden nickels. Mom and dad, thank you both for the countless hours of heartfelt conversations you gave me throughout my years. That alone has helped shape me into the woman I am today. You taught me to never quit but re-strategize and know that I might be down but never out. I love you both always and with all my heart. To all five of our adult children and grand baby, I love you all dearly. Especially, our grandbaby Myiah Grace.

Finally, my King, my love, and best friend Coach Tierre L. Berger. Honey, thank you for the unhurried moments, talks, and countless hours of teaching. Thank you for pouring into me the word of The Most High through the Bible and I cannot forget our many "shop talks" that we have. You are my best friend, who happens to be my Husband, and I love you -Coach Jacquelyn "Bird" Berger.

Thankful to be under the power of The Most High's grace, mercy, and truth.

*Jude 1:24-25*

[24] Now unto him that is able to keep you from falling, and to present you faultless in the presence of his glory, with exceeding joy,

[25] To the only wise God our Savior, be glory and majesty, dominion and power, both now and forever. Amen.

I want to begin by thanking the powers of heaven: the Father, the Son, and the Holy Spirit. For it was The Most High God, the Great 'I Am that I Am' who guided me as I wrote this book. It is the name He gave to Moses (Exodus 3:14,15). I am grateful to Him for sending His dear Son, our Savior, Yashaya, whom the world calls Jesus Christ.

In ancient Phoenician Hebrew, this name is Ahayah, pronounced AH-HA-YAH, Asher Ahayah. I thank Him for giving me the idea to write this book. In addition to, providing the method, materials, and means to make it possible.

I'm also eternally grateful to a few key people.

First and foremost, I am thankful to my wife and my love: Coach Jacquelyn E. Berger, for working alongside me and providing research and her input. I still don't know how I got so blessed to have such a wonderful, smart, and intelligent woman for all these years. Here we are, twenty-nine years later, and it still feels like yesterday, when we first met at Long Branch Park in Killeen, TX.

I also want to thank my huge supporters: my mom, Elizabeth, and my late dad, (R.I.P) Paul L. Berger Jr., for their love and belief in all my projects. They have stood by me whether they understood my work or not. I attribute and dedicate most of this book to the many conversations I've had with them and the memories I've made with two of the greatest people in my life, my mom and dad.

# Preface

We are programmed very early in life that losing an endeavor or coming in 2nd, 3rd, or even 4th place equates to failure. Yet, we find that true prosperous and wealthy people have had to embrace the word "failure." It is important to experience and understand its meaning many times on the journey of successful living. This book is designed to be a reference guide on dealing with failure and making it through those challenging times in a productive manner.

It's not a get-rich-quick manual, nor is it a pie-in-the-sky remedy. It is a realistic, ten-toes down, systematic process that can be used over and over as often as you experience failure. But before we start, let's clarify a few things.

What does it mean to fail or to have to start over again? To understand what failure is, we must first understand what failure is not.

Failure is not the absence of a successful attempt.

Failure is the absence of ever having tried at all.

People often dream of a perfect relationship. They might wish to accomplish a worthy cause, pursue a goal, or achieve anything significant in life, but they don't do it for fear of failing or messing things up. This means they have already failed by omission because they didn't even try!

All of us have greatness inside us, around us, and upon us. It is up to us to seize that greatness, capture it, nurture it, protect it, and give it time to grow, so it can manifest something bigger and better into our lives.

I believe that we are programmed to do something unique with our lives from birth, and because of that, we must not be afraid to fail. I have experienced numerous incidents of what most people would call "failure" in my life. There were times when I didn't think I would make anything special of myself and believed that bad things would keep happening to me.

I had to face job losses, bankruptcy, and homelessness. I struggled with the deaths of loved ones like most of us have as we grow older. It just didn't seem fair, and I didn't feel like my dreams of having a better life would ever become a reality. I started thinking that maybe they were just distant dreams, never to be accomplished.

One of my dreams was to be in a position where I could help people by adding value and purpose to their lives. I wanted to help enrich and strengthen relationships that were failing due to missed opportunities or miscommunications. I've read books on improved communication, studied various aspects of relationships, attended seminars, and learned about the building blocks of a marriage as well as any other relationship.

I had the knowledge and information, but there was one problem with all that – me. How could I help others when I needed help myself? Why did I feel like I was always losing, always at a deficit, or under pressure? It seemed I was fighting just to stay above water.

I can remember a time in one of the lowest moments of my life when I overheard two gentlemen in a department store. One man said to the other, "I'm so far in debt that getting back to zero would make me happy." To offer support and show his friend that he wasn't alone, the other guy replied, "Well, I'm past broke, my brother. I'm destitute, and that means I'd have to save up even to just be broke."

When I heard how broke, busted, and disgusted with life and circumstances these two men were, I wondered, how could someone be encouraged by listening to all this negativity? This kind of talk was hardly supportive and wouldn't help fix anything!

I felt like I could identify with it, but I did not want to accept this as the outcome for my life. I'm pretty sure I could have chimed in on how rough, tough, and seemingly terrible my present situation was – which would have easily made them feel better about their situation. But I kept my mouth shut. The lesson I learned at that moment, which was quite powerful, was that there was power in just staying quiet. I remember what my parents taught me, and I'm pretty sure all of us have heard it at one point or another, "If you don't have something good to say, don't say anything at all."

As a young man, I would constantly get notions to keep going despite all the setbacks I was experiencing. I kept trying and believing that there was life better than the one I was currently experiencing. I just had to reach it.

I kept pushing forward, doing my best to pursue the direction I wanted my life to go in. I knew what I wanted my life to become, but despite that, I somehow kept making the wrong decisions and the wrong moves. I'd say the wrong things, and eventually, I started to feel its depressive effect on me. I felt like the world's biggest failure.

I particularly remember lying on the floor late one night, staring at the ceiling, wishing to be in a better place than I was currently in. Most people around me would've never thought I was struggling. After all, on the outside, it looked like everything was fine, and I was successful. I had the clothes, the haircut, the posture, and even the walk – just like I had read in most motivational books.

But something was missing. I was missing a vital element in my pursuit of fulfillment. Looking back, I now understand that to feel fulfilled, we need something deeper, much deeper, than just looking successful. The world's definition of success is seriously flawed, and I didn't want to look successful anymore. I didn't want to look like I had it all together. I wanted to actually BE together. I wanted to BE completely whole. I remember praying to the Lord, asking for help and guidance in my life. I asked Him to help me become a better person and show me what I was missing.

On that night, I had a moment of clarity as I laid on the floor. I looked over to my left, and I noticed my old computer. I think it was a Dell, to be exact. I don't know why but I kept focusing on the on and off button. For no reason, I just kept staring at it. I began to think about how convenient it was that computers possessed a built-in mechanism to shut down the whole system if they froze, got stuck, or couldn't compute certain tasks.

When a computer gets overloaded, there is a button to shut it all down completely and just walk away. Then I noticed that the same little button is used to carry out another task – reset! Could it be that this action was my answer?! Should I do it again? Start over?

To reset is to start something again in hopes of a more successful result. In other words, it's an inside job. What would happen if I reset my thoughts?

What would happen if I fed myself positive affirmations, not the negative ones that I had become all too familiar with? I once heard a pastor say, "To win you have to win within before you can win outwardly." This means that there must be a mental shift in you and the things you say to yourself.

I really wanted to win, so I pretended I had an imaginary reset button like a computer. I'd only allow myself to lend an ear to positivity, hoping that in time all my mistakes would be erased, and all my past failures would no longer exist.

Wouldn't it be amazing if we could start over when we're stuck or hit a roadblock? What if we could just restart whenever things got messy in life? What if we could hit the reset button and suddenly know what to do and how to get un-slumped? You could now move through it and get to the next part of your life! You could just try it again and hopefully not get stuck this time!

All you had to do was reset and try it again. Reset your mind to believing that you can start again! When you find yourself in uncomfortable moments, this is when you really get to learn more about yourself. You find out who you are, the strengths that you have, your resilience, and your intestinal fortitude. It is at that moment you must ask yourself the most powerful, gut-level, and honest question, "Is it worth it? Is it worth having to start over again? Can I recover and get it right this time?" And the answer to this is a resounding, "Yes, it is, and you can!"

"Until one is committed, there is hesitancy, the chance to draw back, always ineffectiveness. Concerning all acts of initiative (and creation), there is one elementary truth, the ignorance of which kills countless ideas and splendid plans: that the moment one definitely commits oneself, then Providence moves too. All sorts of things occur to help one that would never otherwise have occurred. A whole stream of events issues from the decision, raising in one's favour all manner of unforeseen incidents and meetings and material assistance, which no man could have dreamt would have come his way.

I have learned a deep respect for one of Goethe's couplets:
Whatever you can do, or dream you can, begin it.
Boldness has genius, power, and magic in it!"

— William Hutchison Murray

# Chapter 1 - Believe That You Can

For many years, it was believed that you had to be very lucky, super-intelligent or already wealthy to succeed. I've realized that although there are people with the above factors who are successful, you don't need any of it. You need to have a particular mindset and attitude of never giving up, never caving in, and never quitting, which is a characteristic of every goal-oriented and triumphant individual.

There is another characteristic coursing through the veins of well-accomplished people; They aren't afraid to do it. Even in the face of failure, you can't be afraid to start again. You can't let a fear of failure hold you back.

The word "failure" has haunted many people to paralysis. We end up not trying at all or become increasingly reluctant and slow about starting again and re-engaging our most laudable undertakings. Staying on this path will eventually take you to a place where you won't take any action and will become afraid of even trying. God, forbid we try something and not get the outcome we desire instantly. We quickly revert to labeling it as a failure and let negativity take over our minds, telling us that it must not have been meant for us. This negative mentality will only intensify the belief system that you couldn't have done it in the first place.

Most of us think so negatively about ourselves because we've been told "No!" or "You can't" thousands of times throughout our lives. By the time we're eight-teen, we mostly begin to form a subconscious belief about ourselves that states that we can't achieve it, so we shouldn't even try. We start putting limits or barriers on what is attainable for us. If you put limits on what you can do, you put limits on what you will do! Often, it is far below our true and unlimited potential that The Most High God has given us.

Today, most of us would agree without argument that the potential of the human brain is infinite. Thus, it is overly generous to state that a person uses 10%, 5%, or even 1% of their potential brain capacity. We need to recondition our minds to the possibility of accomplishment. We can only achieve what we envision ourselves achieving. Here is something you should never forget: If any man or woman has accomplished it in life, you can too. You can be the first even if no man or woman has done it. It's all a matter of what you believe. You must look past your negativity and the mental programming you've been inundated with and trust that the Lord has created you for a purpose.

According to a T.D.A Lingos research report called 'Dormancy of the Human Brain,' we only use 10% of our brain and only 10% of our potential. This is infinitely optimistic, as I believe that it is much less. We can achieve anything if we want to.

Let's examine the "why" for a moment. Why do you want to achieve this? What is it all for? If you're money-driven, and that's why you want to be successful, your purpose has not been released yet, because money is the last part of the journey, not the first.

The Bible makes it simple in *Proverbs 23:4-5*:

(4) Labor not to be rich: cease from thine own wisdom.

(5) Wilt thou set thine eyes upon that which is not? For riches certainly make themselves wings; they fly away as an eagle toward heaven.

In other words, don't work or wish to be successful so you can become rich, because you will not feel fulfilled by it. Your fulfillment comes from knowing your purpose in life and your life's worth. Moreover, you won't be able to sustain it because you did it to get money and not follow your passion.

It is the equivalent of wanting to be a doctor because they make good money instead of wanting to help people and save lives. See the difference? In one instance, the motivation was money; In the other, it was the purpose. They both can make money. However, only one can be sustained and make it past any setbacks and hurdles that life throws. This is because of the purpose and not the paper (money). Generally, the paper follows the purpose anyway, so find your why and fly!

## Dealing with Negative Naysayers

Naysayer = A person who only has negative things to say to you or about you.

Naysayers: we know them by name, don't we? They are the ones who might mean well when they say things like, "I just don't want you to get hurt," "Those are just dreams," and, "It didn't work for me and I don't want you to go through that kind of disappointment," or even "You're just wasting your time because that project will never work," and even, "You can't repair that marriage, it's too far gone." If you think about it, naysayers tend to speak from their apprehension about what they can achieve. They tend to transfer the same negativity onto you, sometimes not even realizing the damage they're causing.

Naysayers tend to speak from their view on what they have achieved for themselves. So, the only reference is themselves. Be extremely careful when you talk to a naysayer. You should never pour your heart out to them or tell them any formal, intricate details of your dreams, ideas, desires, and purpose.

Always be brief and use language that's assuring without wavering. The minute they sense that you're unsure of your direction, that's when all hell is going to break loose. They're going to tell you how difficult your dreams and ideas are, how you failed in relationships and can't recover them, etc. By the time they've finished giving you all the reasons why you won't succeed, you're going to feel like your dreams and ideas are stupid. You will leave feeling that there is no point in even trying because you will surely fail.

Most naysayers don't mind you being successful as long as you're less successful than they are.

The art of doing it again is sometimes painful. We, by nature, tend to avoid all aspects of it. Who wouldn't, right? But the point that most of us miss is that although the process is painful, sometimes there is a lesson to be learned through the "doing it again" process.

The reality is that while some people learn to grow, change, adapt and eventually soar high as they go through experiences of doing it again, others go through the same thing but end up crashing and burning. There are several reasons why this happens:

1. They get angry.

2. They blame others.

3. They become bitter.

4. They resent.

5. They grow jealous.

6. They give up.

7. They accept not doing it again!

Don't avoid pain; Learn to deal with it. Don't avoid people; Learn to deal with them.

Find out what lessons you are learning from this experience. Get back up and do it again. Get back in the race and build yourself up from the setback you encountered. After all, now you know what not to do, which is just as good as knowing what to do. Now do it again!

Most individuals don't realize what I'm about to plainly reveal to you. You cannot be successful without having a purpose. This means that success only occurs as a result of knowing your purpose. Sometimes, you experience setbacks, which can be major or minor. You will learn what purpose truly feels and looks like when it happens. Notice and absorb the small victories; For example, if you want to start a business, a small victory would be found in determining the name of your business. Next would be to go downtown to obtain your DBA, which is a business license.

I read an article once about people who win the lottery. They get this enormous windfall of money, and no matter what amount is given, if they haven't done their internal learning of the relationship between their purpose and money, they will invariably lose it all within a few short years. Research shows that a significant number of lottery winners lose all their winnings within five years, as reported by Stephen Goldbart, a psychologist and Co-director of the Money Meaning and Choice Institute in Kentfield. He offers advice to people who come into financial windfalls. It's clear that understanding the principles of purpose becomes necessary for all areas of life. Here are the fundamental principles that will help you on your journey to "doing it again":

1. **Get a vision and have a dream**: Have a clear picture of exactly what you want to achieve or do again. Always keep this picture at the top of your mind. Doing something you are passionate about will motivate you to succeed. It all starts with your heart.

2. **Believe**: Believe without a shadow of a doubt that you can do it. Believe against doubt that you will succeed. Believe in The Most High who is helping you get what you want. Stay away from naysayers as well as negative influences like the internet, books, articles, television, games, etc. They will drain your precious time and fill your mind with unproductive thoughts and negativity, making you doubt your ability to succeed. Surround yourself with like-minded people and things that remind you of your potential.

3. **Take responsibility**: Realize that you are responsible for what you do in your life. You alone are responsible for the outcomes of your efforts. Don't look for anyone to blame; feel free to ask for help when needed. Pray, and remember the final decision is up to you; It's your life, after all.

4. **Practice mental conditioning**: Start forming positive habits and make a habit of saying out loud what you hope to achieve. Speak to yourself in an affirming manner. For example, instead of saying, "I'll get it together one day," say, "I'm getting it together today." If you feel awkward speaking out loud to yourself, write it down and then read it a few times. Better yet, re-write it several times each day. Writing down something this powerful is like speaking to a psychiatrist on paper. This helps keep you centered on your goals. It also builds your self-belief, self-esteem, and confidence.

5. **Make a commitment and stick to it:** Whether it's enriching your relationships, marriage, or even your purpose, make a firm commitment to action. Decide to take whatever steps you need to help you achieve your goals, then honor your commitment. Too often, we find it easy to keep our commitments to others while neglecting to uphold the commitments we make to ourselves. This pattern must change if you want to succeed in doing it again.

6. **Make it concrete:** Cement in what you want to achieve. You need to make it concrete by setting your goals. Your goals must be specific, measurable, motivating, attainable, and attractive. Most importantly, they have got to be realistic. Put a time frame on when you want to achieve them for good measure.

7. **Act:** If you are to do it again, work out a plan of action. Break down the plan and take baby steps to achieve it. Remind yourself that each step you take brings you closer to your goals and perform these steps to the best of your abilities. Fill your days with faith, determination, and purpose to reach your goal, and most importantly, be consistent. After all, you can devour a whole whale if you take, one bite at a time.

8. **Have persistence power:** Do not give up on doing it again until you have achieved what you desire. Be willing to change the parts of your plan that don't bring in the results you seek and adapt yourself to achieve success. It has been said that Thomas Edison did not give up on his quest to invent the lightbulb even though he failed over 10,000 times; Now, that's persistence! See, every failure is a steppingstone towards achieving your life's goals. It is merely a temporary setback, so you must make a comeback, learn from it, and push on towards your goal. All things considered; It is your dream. So go and do it again.

9. **Be grateful**: Maintain an attitude of gratitude, thanking The Most High above for giving you a purpose, a dream, a desire, and a vision. Be grateful that God trusted you with this idea and refuse to complain. Be grateful for where you are now and where you are headed. Look around for things to be grateful for. You'll be surprised at what you find.

10. **Become a giver**: Tithe to your church or donate to charity for example. Giving to worthy causes adds value to your present relationships. As you form new relationships, always think about what you can do for other people. Remember, what goes around comes around. Over time, whatever dreams you have will most likely involve interacting with other people. So, be kind and generous to all. You never know where or when your breakthrough will come.

If life knocks you down, try your best to land on your back, because if you can look up, you can get up!

~Les Brown.

# Chapter 2 - Do it Again, Quickly

Why is it essential to master the art of doing it again? The answer is simple: You want to recover from failure as quickly as possible. Time is of the essence, and it can be on your side if you don't squander it. Seize the moment and make it your own. If you've been hurt, disappointed, or suffered serious setbacks in life, then it's a good way to absorb that hurt and use it to propel your mission forward.

Sure, it may take a little time to gather yourself when you've been hit with a devastating loss or a setback. It may be from the death of a loved one, the loss of a job, the end of a relationship, or any other change that alters life as you know it.

Losing a loved one, a job, or a relationship tends to hit you differently than losing a purpose or an endeavor.

Grief is a process not a task, so take time for this process. Sometimes, the loss can feel unreal, empty, and lonely. We say things like: "I shouldn't have...," "I wish I...," or "If only I...."

There are various stages of grief that we may go through, seven to be exact: shock, denial, anger, bargaining, depression, testing, and finally acceptance. I will not go into the specific details of the seven stages, you can research them if need be. After you've hit these stages, the key is to get back up and bravely face the reality of what happened. Once you learn to accept what happened and let it go, you become armed with the wisdom of knowing what worked and what didn't.

If you neglect to start or restart the journey towards your purpose, you will resign yourself to being stuck in a routine caused by fear. Fear will paralyze you into not moving forward, which will leave you in a bad place.

Here's a true story, once I took a job in the deli section of a particular grocery store. I quickly became friends with a guy named Steve, who also worked in the deli section.

As time passed, I can remember how Steve and I would take lunch breaks together. We often talked about creating a better life for ourselves. We even discussed details about how we would do it. I recall how much I admired Steve's vision of what he would do. I thought to myself, *I should get a better plan because Steve has his life plans sorted out.* We often joked about how we were going to resign from our present jobs and finally work on our own plans.

The more we held this discussion the more dramatic its ending became. Much like Clark Gable's performance in the movie "Gone with The Wind," our discussions were seasoned with flair and humorous creativity. It reminded me of the scene in which Clark Gable would respond to the female co-stars' whims. I've always had an artistic ability for dramatics anyway.

A few months passed, and I told Steve I was finally leaving. He thought I was joking, as usual, but this time, I didn't follow up with my usual stage play performance of a wild dramatic ending. Steve was finally convinced when he saw that I had turned in my deli vest and hat. I gave him my telephone number so we could keep in touch from time to time. Still stunned by my abrupt departure, he bid me goodbye. Steve wished me luck and told me he'd be leaving soon too. Then he said something that stopped me in my tracks.

You see, Steve was a very articulate and personable man with plenty of charisma. One of the most profound statements I have ever heard him say, was, "We can't allow our lives to drift. We have to drive it." At that point I thought my buddy was headed for a successful life very soon.

As time went on Steve was still working at the same grocery store. Occasionally, I would stop by and catch up with him. He would tell me about how he still wanted to begin the business he often spoke of. Before leaving, he would almost always say to me, "I'm about to do it, man. I'm going to start my business." A few more seasons passed, yet his whereabouts remained the same. Eventually, I got word that Steve was no longer with us. My friend died from heart failure on a bus on his way to the same grocery store. Steve had big dreams and plans, but he played it safe and never experienced doing what he wanted to, because of the fear of failure. He had time but resolved himself to being a deli attendant. My heart was truly broken over the news for a long time. It still hurts when I recall this moment.

As time progresses, I often wonder if Steve truly believed he could do better. I remember how he shared with me the intricate details of what he would do. He had a solid plan. Unfortunately, he never fulfilled it.

Although Steve was promoted to a higher position in the selfsame deli-section-he wanted more. I know he did. What kept him from going for it? For ages, Steve worked for very little money. I know for a fact that he had the potential to make much more if he could have just stopped letting his fear of failure hinder him.

See, it's not at all about the money or the position but rather the purpose. Your purpose will make way for provision. Provision follows purpose. It was evident that was not his purpose because he kept saying he didn't want to be there. He expressed to me, on numerous occasions, that it didn't make him happy. So, what was it that kept him there? It wasn't his passion. It was just a job for him, a way to stay afloat.

On the flip side, if that was what Steve wanted and he was happy working in the deli with a passion for it, things would have been totally different. It's not a job if you love what you do. It's only a job if you don't.

That is one of the world's many mysteries today. Very few understand this, and those who do easily manage to soar high and accomplish a lot in their lives. In the end, nobody can beat you being you! That's right; I'm talking about being authentically you. It's your voice, your style, and your confidence. The way you do things makes you, you. So, embrace it! Don't try to compare yourself to others. Don't be a copy of someone else; Be who you are. In other words, you don't have to compete with anyone. All you must do is create your perfect life.

In creating, you carve out a niche that no one else can duplicate. Sure, they can imitate your style and some of the things you have done, but they can never duplicate it because it is yours. Creativity comes from within. The faster you get comfortable with being you, the quicker you can steer the passion of your purpose. This allows you to start with or re-do what you desire. In the profound words of my late friend, "We can't allow our lives to drift. We have to drive it." Those words continue to play in my mind. Although I must admit, I didn't understand what Steve meant when he first said it; Now, it's crystal clear to me. As a result, in memory of my buddy Steve, I have decided to tell his story in this book. Rest well, my friend.

I firmly believe that if someone takes up the challenge, starts going after their dream, and works on learning the lessons of life, they will inevitably live their dream and purpose. Even if it does not work out, you would be much closer to them than if you had not started. Your gift will make room for you, but you must open the gift to see what's in it.

The journey of a thousand miles begins with one step after another. No matter how big or small you start; Eventually, you get where you're going if you don't stop. Rest if you need to, take a step back, and reevaluate if you must, but never quit. I believe that even if it were Steve's time to depart from this world, he would have left here happier if he would have participated in life fully, lived life on his terms, and with no regrets.

Ralph Waldo Emerson said, "People see only what they are prepared to see." I believe my friend adjusted his dream to look like his present situation, which stops being a dream and becomes a circumstance. Steve only saw himself doing what he was doing because that was all that he prepared his sights for. You and I must see past where we are right now into what we want to become. You can say whatever you want to say in the world, but you will only do what your inner thoughts dictate.

If your mind is not fully convinced of what you want, you won't start moving in that direction. Remember, your present circumstances are not the outcome. If that's not where you want to be, you can reposition yourself by doing it again.

Og Mandino says, "In truth, the only difference between those who have failed and those who have succeeded lies in the difference in their habits. Good habits are the key to all successes, and bad habits are the unlocked doors to failure. Therefore, if I must be a slave to a habit, let me be a slave to a good habit."

My grandfather saved an old record that he let me listen to. Earl Nightingale wrote and recorded a message on that record called "The Strangest Secret" in 1956. Someone asked the professor, "What's wrong with the world today?" The professor thought briefly and replied, "Men don't think." Thinking for yourself is paramount, as it is often said that people are either followers or leaders. It depends on our level of thinking and how we relay those thoughts that dictate what we become.

## A Deeper Look

Does your life feel out of control? Do your stress levels seem to be through the roof? Then maybe it's time for a change – a change in what you think about! What's your self-talk like? The change that we're talking about isn't looking for another crutch or a bandwagon to jump on; be it getting into another dysfunctional relationship or relying heavily on drugs and, or alcohol to get you through the day. This change is about transforming your mindset and living life with a renewed perspective.

Anxiety disorders are the most common mental illnesses in the US and affect about 40 million American adults yearly. Anxiety disorder is also the single biggest clinical risk for the development of depression. The DSM-IV (Diagnostic and Statistical Manual of Mental Disorders), a book written by the American Psychiatric Association, states the following disorders:

**Generalized Anxiety Disorder (GAD)** is a disorder that involves excessive worrying about ordinary day-to-day issues, such as health, money, work, and family.

**Obsessive-Compulsive Disorder (OCD)** is characterized by excessive orderliness, perfectionism, attention to detail, and a need for control in relation to others.

**Panic Disorder (PD)** is characterized by episodic, unexpected panic attacks that occur without a clear trigger.

**Post-Traumatic Stress Disorder (PTSD)** is a disorder that involves flashbacks, nightmares, or uncontrollable thoughts that are triggered by experiencing or witnessing a terrifying event.

**Social Anxiety** is the fear of social situations that involve interaction with other people.

This isn't a comprehensive list, as there are many more categories and conditions of anxiety. If you have been diagnosed with any of the conditions mentioned above and you believe that the Bible is the word of The Most High (God), then it will do you well to examine the scriptures for deeper insight. It may take a little reading, but it will be worth the effort when you notice your anxiety symptoms getting better and feel a stronger connection to God.

*John 5:39 (KJV)*

**39** "Search the scriptures; for in them ye think ye have eternal life: and they are they which testify of me."

The 1611 KJV is the complete Bible in its original form with the Apocrypha. There are more than a few scriptures that aid in dealing with these types of disorders. If you already have the KJV Bible, you can order an Apocrypha online. We recommend the "Authorized (King James) Version" by Red Cambridge University

Press. With this book, coupled with your Bible, you will have the complete Word of the Lord to take guidance from.

I want to take a moment to look at anxiety and depression on the basis of scripture.

*Acts 10:36 - 38 (KJV)*

**36** "The word which God sent unto the children of Israel, preaching peace by Jesus Christ: (he is Lord of all:) 37 That word, I say, ye know, which was published throughout all Judaea, and began from Galilee, after the baptism which John preached; 38 How God anointed Jesus of Nazareth with the Holy Ghost and with power: who went about doing good and healing all that were oppressed of the devil; for God was with him."

We see here that The Most High God anointed Christ, our Lord, and Savior, with the Holy Spirit and power to heal all who were oppressed by evil spirits.

For anyone who has been depressed, feeling "oppressed" is a pretty good description. Emotions become less sharp or absent, energy is depleted, simple tasks become difficult, and everything feels slowed down, apart from your thoughts which seem to be moving faster.

We should also consider anxiety, panic, distress, and hopelessness. Are these emotions a form of "spiritual oppression?" Well, this depends on what you mean by "spiritual." We believe there will be no illness or sickness in heaven, right!? Therefore, to some extent, any kind of sickness is a sign of being unhealthy. It does not come from our Lord and Saviour but a thief at that. At the same time, catching a cold does not immediately mean that a spiritual force is opposing you.

*John 10:10 (NKJV)*

**10** "The thief does not come except to steal, and to kill, and to destroy. I have come that they may have life, and that they may have it more abundantly."

Numbers 11: 1-34 speaks of the Israelites murmuring. They complained and didn't want to be thankful for what The Most High (God) had done for them. They didn't appreciate how he had blessed them and given them His endless bounties.

The number one rule in controlling your anxiety and depression is not to panic! Anxiety and depression are evil spirits that cause you to feel bad. You must realize that depression is a state of being. Most people who are experiencing depression deal with it by seeking therapy from psychologists or trusted professionals in the field. It's all a matter of what you are giving yourself over to.

In the *Apocrypha Ecclesiasticus 30:21*

**21** "Give not over thy mind to heaviness' and afflict not thyself in thine own counsel."

Don't set your mind on heaviness, as it only causes more pain and suffering if you dwell on the negative thoughts in your mind. Don't focus on reasoning with yourself through bad advice, and don't punish yourself with thoughts of anxiety, panic, distress, and hopelessness.

*Psalms 46:10* KJV

"Be still, and know that I am God: I will be exalted among the heathen, I will be exalted in the earth."

Be still, take a breath, and know that He is in control.

*Philippians 4:4 KJV*

"Rejoice in the Lord always and again, I say, Rejoice."

Keep rejoicing in the Lord at all times. To rejoice, you will have to fight for your connection with God. You must ignore the urge to self-sabotage your feelings. It is imperative to have a daily walk with the Lord through prayer and reading the word of God. This keeps you grounded and centered.

*Philippians 4:5 -8 (KJV)*

**5** "Let your moderation be known unto all men. The Lord is at hand.

**6** Be careful of nothing; but in everything by prayer and supplication with thanksgiving let your request be made known unto God.

**7** And the peace of God which passeth all understanding, shall keep your hearts and minds through Christ Yashaya.

**8** Finally, brethren, whatsoever things are true, whatsoever things are honest, whatsoever things are just, whatsoever things are pure, whatsoever things are lovely, whatsoever things are of good report; if there be any virtue, and if there be any praise, think on these things:"

You shouldn't come to the father already defeated. Try to realize that you are in a fight, a spiritual battle for your mind. *It's all in your head*. A victorious mind starts with trusting in The Most High (God). A defeated mind starts with doubting The Most High (God).

Whatever your burden is, give it to the Lord. Christ will keep your heart and mind. He has given us what to think in Philippians 4:8.

*Philippians 4:8 KJV*

8 "Finally, brethren, whatsoever things are true, whatsoever things are honest, whatsoever things are just, whatsoever things are pure, whatsoever things are lovely, whatsoever things are of good report; if there be any virtue, and if there be any praise, think on these things:"

*Psalms 1:1-5 KJV*

1 "Blessed is the man that walketh not in the counsel of the ungodly, nor standeth in the way of sinners, nor sitteth in the seat of the scornful.

2 But his delight is in the law of the Lord; and in his Law doth he meditate day and night.

3 And he shall be like a tree planted by the rivers of water, that bringeth forth his fruit in his season; his leaves also shall not wither, and whatsoever he doeth, shall prosper.

4 The ungodly are not so: but are like the chaff which the wind driveth away.

5 Therefore the ungodly shall not stand in the judgment, nor sinners in the congregation of the righteous."

*3rd John 1:2 KJV*

"Beloved, I wish above all things that thou mayest prosper and be in health, even as thy soul prospereth." One of the most important conditions that we face is the condition of our soul.

What are we giving our minds over to; To prosper and to be healthy not only in body but also in sound mind.

*2 Timothy 1:7 KJV*

"For God hath not given us the spirit of fear; but of power, and of love, and of a sound mind."

A prayer is a form of constant communication with The Most High God. Through his word, you have been given a way of life that is not subject to how you are feeling.

*Roman 1:17 KJV*

"For therein is the righteousness of God revealed from faith to faith: as it is written, The just shall live by faith."

We should never forget to live by faith as it can move mountains in our lives.

Living by faith keeps your mind from freaking out because you believe that everything will be alright. You accept that certain things are beyond your control, and your circumstances may not look like how you want them to all the time, but eventually, everything will work out.

*Psalms 41:1-3 KJV*

**1** "Blessed is he that considereth the poor: the LORD will deliver him in time of trouble.

**2** The LORD will preserve him, and keep him alive; and he shall be blessed upon the earth: and thou wilt not deliver him unto the will of his enemies.

**3** The LORD will strengthen him upon the bed of languishing: thou wilt make all his bed in his sickness."

We need to be patient. When you can't fight the spiritual issues in your body, you might feel stuck, but don't use others as emotional dumpsters. Don't tell social media your problems. There is a lot of uncertainty that comes from not knowing what will happen daily (1st Corinthians 10 and 13).

Whatever it is you are going through, someone else is going through it as well. We put ourselves through things that cause us to panic even more and unravel. We have got to be strong in faith Christ has put us on a straight and narrow path, and we must stay there (*Jeremiah 38:3-11*).

In reading this passage we can see that panic and depression have one thing in common an absence of faith and prayer. The princes panicked in the situation due to the lack of faith and prayer in their lives. On the other hand, the eunuch and the fifty men who lived in prayer and faith responded differently, by speaking up for Jeremiah. Jeremiah was going through trying times because he was speaking what The Most High told him to speak (Daniel 11:33). If you find yourself in the dungeon, daily reliance needs to be on The Most High (God). In Jeremiah we read about his story but in Romans 5:1-5 we see that when we experience these trying times how they work for our good.

Remember, experience plus knowledge equals wisdom.

*Jeremiah 29:11* says, "For I know the thoughts that I think toward you, saith the LORD, thoughts of peace, and not of evil, to give you an expected end." In the Apocrypha, Ecclesiasticus 30:14 says, "Better is the poor, being sound and strong of constitution, than a rich man that is afflicted in his body." Verse 15 says, "Health and good estate of body are above all gold, in a strong body above infinite wealth."

Heavier mental health conditions like bipolar disorder, borderline personality disorder, and schizophrenia require medications, at which a psychiatrist would need to prescribe. They specialize in diagnosing and treating more complex mental health conditions.

It's time to do some critical thinking of your own! Early scholarly literature from Socrates, the teacher of Plato, states, "The unexamined life is not worth living." In simple terms, the unexamined life is likely to come with many regrets and unnecessary stress.

The above statement holds true. If your unexamined habits lead you to try something one day and then quit it the next day, then you would have no other result but failure. Your bad habit of quitting would dictate that.

Maybe you don't get the desired outcome you want the first time. However, as you keep moving towards your goals, you are a "work in progress." A situation considered a failure by one might be seen as a success by another. Such as in the case of direct competition or what is known as "zero-sum."

Generally, a zero-sum is a situation in which a participant's gain or loss is balanced by the other participant's losses or gains. It is called "zero-sum" because when the total gains of the participants are added up and the total losses subtracted, they will sum to zero. So, you basically lose and gain nothing. "Chess" and "Go" are examples of zero-sums.

Both players can win, even though they might have to play through a process where in they are losing game pieces. This may be viewed as a failure in the minds of those who don't understand, howbeit, sometimes you may have to lose pieces to win.

What pieces have you lost in your life that you felt were failures? Looking back, they may have been blessings in disguise, and you've lost nothing. Of course, unfortunately, this doesn't include the loss of a loved one. But even in that, you can find comfort in memories and experiences that will never be forgotten.

You can't allow your life to drift; You must drive it. Examine your life, does it feel empty? Are you busy doing stuff without any direction or purpose? Busyness without purpose and direction creates artificial significance. It satisfies movement, but that movement without a destination will lead to more frustration. Busyness must be more than just doing stuff.

Love is composed of a single soul inhabiting two bodies.

~ Aristotle

# Chapter 3 - Relationship Maintenance

Do you ever wonder what secrets exist in successful marriages that keep couples together for twenty, thirty, and forty plus years?

What about how to recover from being on the brink of a divorce? What does it take to break through the boredom and monotony of a long relationship?

If you are wondering what the big secret is, then you are about to find out!

Let us start by first establishing that there is not a secret to it at all! It is simply having the knowledge to keep things together. It is about knowing what to do and what not to do. This requires both parties to know what to say, when to say, and how to say it.

Having wisdom and knowledge puts you in a seat of confidence and is an important skill that all couples should invest in. It can keep you from fraying or altogether destroying your relationship.

In any relationship, maintenance is required to keep the spark alive. When I say maintenance, I'm talking about keeping the marriage in good functioning condition. Think of how you take your car for regular servicing, even when it's working just fine.

Similarly, **preventive maintenance** is the single most important thing you can do to ensure the longevity of your relationship.

Regular maintenance of your relationship is like getting regular checkups at the family doctor. They keep you healthy and ensure that any medical concerns are diagnosed effectively before they turn into serious conditions.

Open communication in your relationship serves in a similar way. It is a form of preventive maintenance or a doctor's checkup that lets you assess how things are going. After all, there's no way to recognize and correct what has not been assessed and addressed.

In other words, you can't manage what you can't measure.

You can't guess your way through a diagnostic assessment on a vehicle, right? Guessing would be a costly waste of time, especially if you have the tools and equipment needed to do a proper diagnostic. Simply choosing to take a shortcut by guessing or ignoring the problem won't do you any favors.

Sometimes, we may feel like we know what the issue is without having a conversation about it. This causes us to start behaving in ways that fit our thoughts and what we are unclear about. Then, quite naturally, we tend to fill in the gaps (what we don't exactly know) with what we think is wrong.

Prescription without proper diagnosis is malpractice for a reason. You must **know** exactly what's wrong before you can work out an effective solution.

My wife uses the platitude, "I can't get what's in your head unless you give it to me." This simply indicates that people aren't mind readers and, thereby, will not know what issues are troubling their partners unless they express it openly.

Proper communication gives the relationship a chance to catch small problems before they become bigger ones. Each conversation is an opportunity to learn something new about your partner that you didn't know before. Even if the conversation is difficult and uncomfortable to have, ultimately, it will be worth the effort it takes to fully understand your partner and resolve any issues.

## Watch Your Mouth

Pay attention to the words you speak. Are you encouraging or defeating? Do you uplift your partner or bad-mouth them?

Women, how are you talking to and about your husbands?

Men, how are you talking to and about your wives?

Pay attention to what you are saying about them, especially to other people like your friends, co-workers, and associates. Your words give mental images of your mate, and they can form a good or bad persona of them.

Your spouse can only be as great or as terrible as the picture you paint of them with your words. These words can build up or tear down your partner. Therefore, it is far better to speak positive things about them, even if you feel like they are lacking or falling short in regard to something you expected of them.

By focusing on what they are doing right instead of any mistakes or grievances, you can encourage your partner to want to do better and work on their shortcomings.

On the other hand, if you constantly speak negatively and berate them, it will only cause more problems in your relationship. Never saying a kind, thoughtful, or motivating word to your spouse isn't the right way to treat them. How can anybody be expected to stay motivated and encouraged to better themselves if they are belittled and made to feel horrible or look bad around others?

This behavior will only push your partner away, and soon, they, too, will find reasons to speak poorly of you in much the same manner. Two negatives only make a positive in mathematics, never in actual relationships.

For men, lack of communication tends to be a big issue in relationships. We found that most men hope for problems, issues, and bad situations to simply go away or magically fix themselves if they don't acknowledge them or talk about them. They think they won't need to go through the embarrassment of attempting to try discussing it.

This type of thinking is grounded in fear. Men experience fear of miscommunication. They are afraid of their words not coming out right or being unable to express moments appropriately, which only causes more frustration and despair.

These past practices are future indicators of the merry-go-round in which the same routine continues. The man just assumes that his partner will misinterpret what he is really trying to say and maybe even make things worse, thereby never getting to a resolution.

So, when men hear the words "We need to talk" from their partners, they immediately get defensive and do one of three things:

They will immediately run through any possible scenarios of what in the world could be wrong in their mind while trying to remain calm. You'll find that they get angry and eventually lash out or just shut down altogether without saying a word.

A man's defenses kick in when they start to assume, and negative expressions and statements will soon follow.

*"We need to talk."*

Here's a tip for the ladies. When you need to have a serious conversation with your partner, try saying, "Honey, when is a good time we can talk?" Instead of those dreaded four words.

If he asks what it's about, simply reply with, "I would like some time to talk to you, share my thoughts, and hear your opinion about _____."

When the agreed-upon time comes, ladies, this is a very important part; Ask again, "Honey, is it still a good time to talk?"

In doing so, you are respecting him while also reminding him of his promise to give some time to hold the conversation. It also ensures that there is nothing else going on that would warrant his immediate attention. You are respecting his position as the head of the household while also ensuring that your need to have an open and honest conversation is met.

Some men might refuse this tactic and say this will not work for me, and that's fine. Remember, you don't have to know or understand every man, just know yours and how to communicate with him.

*Ephesians 5:20 -22 KJV*

**20** Giving thanks always for all things unto God and the Father in the name of our Lord Jesus (Yashaya) Christ;

**21** Submitting yourselves one to another in fear of (The Most High) God.

**22** Wives, submit yourselves unto your own husbands, as unto the Lord.

When most of us read this passage of scripture, the immediate focus falls on verse 22, where wives are asked to "... submit yourselves unto your own husbands, as unto the Lord."

Submitting means to accept or yield yourself to a superior force or to the authority or will of another person. So, by definition, the last part of the submission is about submitting to the will of another person or yielding.

Verse 21 talks of submitting yourselves **one to another** in fear of (The Most High) God. There is a level of submitting yourselves, **one to another,** between a husband and wife, which includes consideration, changing your mind, compromise, and negotiation. It is a formula where the husband listens to the wife's input and honestly considers it if it makes sense. Similarly, the wife should not yield to anyone but her husband as unto the Lord. Submitting to one another is done through communication and understanding.

For example, in marriage there are certain things you do that your spouse may not like or approve of. You need to listen, understand, and submit to that wish or request. A small example is hugging other women full-on. Most, if not all, women have objections to seeing their men hugging other women or being hugged by them.

This action makes most women suspicious and uncomfortable. Suspicious in the sense that women know other women, and some hugs are not what they seem. Some embraces are straight carnal in nature to get a feel or to send a nonverbal message in the other person's mind of lustful things.

In being aware of the other women's devices, the wife may caution her husband and request that he not do that action or modify how he does it.

Men - is that the right time to say, *"I don't need to listen to you! I'm the head, and you need to submit to me, not me to you!?"*

Absolutely not!

If you want peace and you want to remain married in a healthy relationship, then it may be a good idea to submit to the request. The point here is that there will be times for submitting one to another, and both parties should do so as needed.

*Ephesians 5:23-31 KJV*

**23** For the husband is the head of the wife, even as Christ is the head of the church: and he is the savior of the body.

**24** Therefore as the church is subject unto Christ, so let the wives be to their own husbands in everything.

**25** Husbands, love your wives, even as Christ also loved the church and gave himself for it;

**26** That he might sanctify and cleanse it with the washing of water by the word,

**27** That he might present it to himself a glorious church, not having spot, or wrinkle, or any such thing; but that it should be holy and without blemish.

**28** So ought men to love their wives as their own bodies. He that loveth his wife loveth himself.

**29** For no man ever yet hated his own flesh; but nourisheth and cherisheth it, even as the Lord the church:

**30** For we are members of his body, of his flesh, and of his bones.

**31** For this cause shall a man leave his father and mother, and shall be joined unto his wife, and they two shall be one flesh.

Husbands, remember that you are responsible for cultivating your wives. To cultivate is to break up the soil in preparation for sowing or planting. It also means to nurture and encourage.

In the case of your relationship, mental thoughts, beliefs, attitudes, how you dress, speak, and conduct business are all forms of cultivation.

When we ask The Most High for a perfect woman to marry, he never gives us a finished product. He gives you seeds, tools, and access to real estate (land) to break up the ground and plant your desired positive qualities into your woman.

Suppose I was an art teacher, and you were a student who wanted to paint a picture for your living room that would include all your favorite colors. It wouldn't be wise of me to paint the picture for you. Sure, I could do it, but it wouldn't resemble exactly what you had in mind, which may be frustrating in the long run, because it's not what you wanted, although I included all the colors you asked for.

On the contrary, if I give you the resources needed to paint, like a canvas, pencils, erasers, paintbrushes, and paint. Then, it is up to you to paint to your heart's desire and create a final product that exactly resembles what you want for the living room.

The scriptures mentioned below offer a blueprint on how to cultivate your wives. You must see her as the softer side of you.

*Verse 29:*

"For no man ever yet hated his own flesh; but nourisheth and cherisheth it, even as the Lord the church.

To cultivate your wife, you must spend deliberate quality time with her. This is not done by just "making time" for her but also by "taking time" for her. Instead of trying to fit your "together" time within your free hours try taking time for her by calling off work every now and then just to spend the day together. Have fun, plan activities, and plug into each other.

While spending this precious time together, be sure to encourage her, protect her, show affection towards her, and most importantly share the word of The Most High (Bible) with her.

Bible studies together teach and correct you both. Let the word of God speak, and in so doing, you may be able to cultivate good things in her that she may not be aware of.

Sharing religious studies with your wife will help you strengthen, encourage, help her take notice of herself, and become an even better version of who she is, for herself and you.

Conversely, every time you criticize your partner by putting the fault on them, using scripture to hold your power over them, attack, blame, and inject negative statements like, "You're always running late," or "You never do anything right" you are only making things worse for her and yourself. This is not cultivating at all. In fact, instead of breaking up her ground to plant good seeds, you're planting more of the same spoiled seeds that you complain about.

The words "Always" and "Never" are absolutes and shouldn't be said in a conversation because then it's not a fair statement.

For example, saying, "you **NEVER** take out the garbage, I **ALWAYS** have to do it!" can be argued as un-true because what you are really saying is that since the time you and your spouse were born, they have **NEVER** touched a trash can, and you have **ALWAYS** taken out the garbage. This includes the time you both didn't even know each other. So, can you really say they have **NEVER** done it, and you **ALWAYS** have? Think about it.

Saying always and never leaves gaps in effective communication and can corrode your relationship. Instead, say something like, "I feel unheard by you when I ask if you could take out the garbage, and you don't do it."

By being defensive and refusing to accept responsibility or attacking in response to feedback from your partner, you chip away the trust and goodwill in your marriage. If you have an attitude of contempt, call your partner names, or make stinging, sarcastic remarks, you imply that you're superior and your partner is below you.

Every time you stone-wall one another or emotionally beat each other up, you both shut down instead of openly addressing the issues. By shutting down, you create more distance and dishonesty in the relationship rather than openness, communication, and love.

Men, the next time you hear, "We need to talk" from your spouse, see it as an opportunity to listen and negotiate a solution. What men need to understand is that when a woman says she wants to talk, she's telling you that she wants to feel closer to you. The only way to achieve this connection and closeness is through effective communication.

Unfortunately, most men have not built a strong muscle in the skill of communicating effectively, especially when it comes to expressing themselves in relationships. Words don't quite come out right, or what was said and understood was not how it was meant at all.

So, when a man hears the statement, "We need to talk," he immediately thinks something is wrong. He gets queasy butterflies in his stomach, becomes defensive, and then angry because it's going to be a long night.

Nevertheless, instead of dreading this conversation, men should use it to do a maintenance checkup on their relationship. Embrace the talk and know that everything is not doom and gloom.

Take your time and gather your thoughts; There is no rush! Think twice, speak once, run it through your mind, and then try to rephrase that thought in a loving way without any hostility or venom.

According to a recent study by the American Academy of Matrimonial Lawyers (AAML), communication problems were the number one reason for divorce in the United States. The study stated that about 67.5 percent of all marriages failed because of a breakdown of communication. The reasons for this severe lack of communication include arguing, the inability to understand your spouse, or a total absence of communication.

We're born alone, we live alone, and we die alone. Only through our love and friendship can we create the illusion for the moment that we're not alone.

~ **Orson Welles**

# Chapter 4 - Building the Muscle of Communication

The communication muscle is built through practice. Just like lifting weights in a gym, to build muscle, you need to place enough stress on them to force them to adapt.

Sure, your body may be sore from the workout, but after a while, the awkward soreness and discomfort will no longer be a problem.

Building the muscle of communication looks like this:

**1. Be an Active Listener**. Don't be lazy by just hearing your partner so you can respond or use selective hearing to pick out words to debate on. You should be listening actively and attentively to your spouse. Pay close attention to what they are saying and clarify any vagueness before you form your own conclusions about it.

**2. Be Concise.** Say your message in as few words as possible and get straight to the point. Try not to ramble, as this may cause the listener to tune you out or even avoid speaking to you at all. If you're all over the place when trying to express yourself, nobody will be able to understand you.

**3. Use Body Language.** Body language or non-verbal communication is just as important in the communication process as your words. Start practicing good body language by being relaxed, using eye contact, implementing hand gestures, and paying attention to the tone and cadence of your voice while talking.

**4. Be confident.** Having confidence in what you say and how you communicate will ensure that your interaction comes across genuine and authentic. Maintaining eye contact shows that you are confident. Also, try to avoid sounding aggressive or belittling.

**5. Have an open mind.** You may find it hard to agree with what's being said, but even then, try to sympathize. Do your best to understand their point of view rather than simply trying to get your message across first. Remember, seek to understand before being understood.

**6. Be respectful**. Being respectful can be as easy as giving your undivided attention through eye contact and head nods. Include their name while speaking from time to time, so they realize that you are focused on them, and they will feel appreciated and heard.

By placing your communication skills under the required tension through intentional practice, you can build your communication muscles easily. Practice expressing yourself, practice listening, just practice, practice, practice.

If you are terrible at communicating, you may have to start by writing down what you wish to say first and then practice saying it. You can even do this in front of a mirror!

Communication maintenance boosts safety and security in relationships. One of the primary reasons for building good communication skills is to create a safe environment in a thriving relationship. Communication maintenance also maintains the value of your relationship. There is a noticeable difference between a well-maintained relationship and one that is neglected. A well-maintained relationship is easy to spot as it will have honor, respect, realistic expectations, trust, boundaries, and no violence for one another.

On the other hand, an unkempt relationship is one that has obvious signs of neglect.

Lastly, communication maintenance lowers your running costs. It doesn't take as much effort to "get down the road" together when you spend deliberate quality time and understand each other's wants and needs. Just like a vehicle, the better it is maintained, the lesser it costs to fix should the need ever arise.

Now let's hear from my wife, Coach Jacquelyn Berger, about strengthening and building relationships.

## Strengthening and Building Your Relationship

### From Coach Jacquelyn Berger

Thank you, sweetheart.

In building a relationship, ladies, a safe practice to use is what I like to call the **Guiding Principles.** These principles were set in place by The Most High God.

We must understand that building a friendship within your relationship is one of these guiding principles. You might ask, what truly is friendship, and why does it play an important role?

Friendship is a relationship that is built on trust, compassion, honesty, and involves complete investment in one another. It includes care and concern. A true friend is rare, and when you find one, you should always honor that relationship.

In thinking about friendships, we can use the analogy of the virtuous woman. Scriptures read:

*Proverbs 31:10 KJV*

"Who can find a virtuous (rare) woman for her price is far above rubies."

The Lord loves when husbands and wives agree. The word "agree" simply means that he loves when husbands and wives are of one accord. Examples of this would include agreement in regard to matters like child-rearing, saving money, and dealing with the cares of this life.

The Bible says:

*Proverbs 18:22 KJV*

"Whoso findeth a wife findeth a good thing."

When it says findeth, this means he was seeking a good wife, and she had the attributes of being that. She understands how important friendship and integrity are to the relationship. Most importantly, she has done the internal work to be a good wife.

She has learned to be temperate in her mind and body. She speaks with kindness, isn't lazy, has moral excellence, etc.

Remember, ladies, a man **finds**, but a woman is **chosen**. So, make sure you are doing the internal work to become the chosen one. In understanding that a man finds a wife, ladies, you might be looking (watching and praying) for a faithful man.

Remember the steps (lifestyle) of a good man are ordered by God. In deciding if this man is the one for you, ask yourself if he is able to take care of you physically, emotionally, and financially. Check to see if he is following Biblical principles for marriage. Can he lead and cover you?

These concepts are very important when you are trying to build a relationship. People often say that buying a house is one of the biggest investments you will ever make in your life. While this may be true, I don't think it is the "biggest" investment. The biggest decision you will make in your life is who you marry.

Marriage was designed to be a lifelong commitment. It is not something that should be taken lightly or done haphazardly. So, men, when you are choosing your wife, choose wisely. Make sure that she knows and understands your vision, how to follow you, and help build a legacy with you that you can be proud of.

In a marital relationship, you will have challenges. These tests and trials come along to make your relationship strong. When they come knocking on your doorstep, it is a test of how you both will handle them. It is a challenge to your relationship.

The best way to handle these challenges is to first seek to understand before being understood. In other words, it is more important to gain an understanding from your partner than it is for you to assert yourself before knowing what's going on in their minds.

Also, you are showing that you humbly give up the need to be right. Saying what you didn't like or want before you have even heard their side can cause frustration and animosity. The Bible says:

*Proverbs 4:7 KJV*

"Wisdom is the principal thing; therefore, get wisdom: and with all thy getting understanding."

It's sad that in some relationships, wives need to make an appointment to see their own husbands. Men, are your wives among them?

She wants to see you, and you haven't talked to her properly for months! I'm not speaking of having a conversation about bills or the children. Besides these mundane responsibilities, are you actively engaging with your wife? You are the manager of your home, and therefore, it's important for you as a man to understand that the family is your most sacred responsibility.

## Feed the Courage, Starve the Fear

The nugget of wisdom that was given to me years ago by my father was, "Feed what you want to live, starve what you want to die in your life."

It's a universal statement that shows a person that whatever they feed or neglect to feed produces the outcome they assigned to it. It means that whatever you're feeding in your life right now is what is becoming stronger; whether it's addiction, neglect, or love.

If you are feeding your relationship with neglect, insecurity, lies, and unfaithfulness, then those actions will gain more strength and take over. The relationship will suffer and die due to malnutrition, and you will only feel more distant from your partner.

Let's say you want to literally give up smoking, but you keep buying cigarettes. Are you feeding that addiction or starving it? That's right. You're feeding it!

Figuratively, if you feed your addictions or your habits with more of the same, they will only become stronger. The opposite of feeding is starving. When you feed one area of your life, you must be aware that you are automatically starving the other area. Feeding love, honor, and respect to your relationship automatically starves out hate, dishonor, and contempt.

Continue to, or perhaps revive, your courtesies of courtship in your married life. Successful marriages don't just happen; they need to be developed. It is not always the big things that make a difference; the little things count just as much. If we continue to remind ourselves to pay attention to the small details in our marriages that matter, then we will find that the bigger issues are handled quite easily.

**Don't take each other for granted**.

Remember what it took to get him or her. It is going to take that and a little more creativity to keep them.

*1 Peter 4:8 (KJV)*

"And above all things have fervent charity (love) among yourselves: for charity(love) shall cover the multitude of sins."

Also,

*Proverbs 31:28 (KJV)*

**(MEN)** "Her children arise up, and call her blessed; her husband also, and he praiseth her." Her husband praises her!

In order to praise her, you must take notice of her, and you won't do so if you take her for granted.

Likewise (**WOMEN**), remember to show reverence and respect to your husband, calling to mind:

*Colossians 3:18 (KJV)*

"Wives, submit yourselves unto your own husbands, as it is fit in the Lord."

**Feed what you want to live in your marriage and starve what you want to die out of your marriage.**

Keep love growing by expressing affection for one another, or it will die, and you will drift apart. Love and happiness are not found by seeking them for yourself but rather by giving them to each other.

**Take time for each other.**

Notice we didn't say "MAKE TIME" we said "TAKE TIME" because they are two different things. Taking time is intentional. You purposely take out time for your spouse.

Throughout our day, with the hustles and bustles of life and all the daily stressors, we seem to run out of time for our spouses. If you find that you barely see your spouse, decide upon a day for you both to call off from work, cancel appointments, and put the phone on silent mode. Plug into one another. Spend this time fully devoted to each other and learn as much as possible about each other. Do fun things together, and you will eventually learn how to get along well.

It is very important that we learn to greet each other with enthusiasm and love. So, relax, visit, shop, sight-see, pray, and eat together, remembering to never overlook the small things.

Try to "out-love" each other, and don't take more out of the marriage than you put into it. Think of how you make consistent deposits into your bank account in hopes of increasing your savings. Similarly, make deposits in the form of time, love, commitment, and affection into your relationship account so that if you ever need to make a withdrawal, you will have adequate funds to do so.

An overdraft happens when we haven't kept a check on how much we are depositing into the relationship. When we try to resolve it through guessing and hoping, things never work out, and you might end up taking more than you have put in - leading to hefty debts that can weigh down on your relationship.

The Most High loves when husbands and wives agree. How you both decide to do this, the way you walk together, and the things you agree on, are all a part of your relationship-building too.

Men were designed to be motivated by sight, so they focus most on what they **SEE**. On the other side, women were created to be motivated by what they **HEAR.**

Speak affirming words of encouragement as much as possible to your wife. Your lady depends on your words being lively and encouraging. Offer her words full of love, reassurance, and focus.

Similarly, women should remember that their husbands are motivated by sight. The best way to express your love is to **SHOW** them. Give them something to see and feel.

*Ephesians 4:2-6 (KJV)*

(2) With all lowliness and meekness, with longsuffering, forbearing one another in love;

(3) Endeavoring to keep the unity of the Spirit in the bond of peace.

(4) There is one body, and one Spirit, even as ye are called in one hope of your calling;

(5) One Lord, one faith, one baptism,

(6) One God and Father of all, who is above all, and through all, and in you all.

We are being called to become single and be a part of one complete entity. This means singleness in purpose, singleness in our worship of The Most High, not idols, and singleness in the attention we give to our spouse.

On this wise, I think it would be safe to say your marriage is only as good as your ability to form a single connection with your spouse. The following passage in Ephesians 4:4-6 uses the word "one" quite often. It shows how people are many but refers to it as becoming one (in body and soul) to live fruitful lives.

In such a case, we need to view our spouse as a part of us, an extension of ourselves that requires us to be completely humble and gentle. They need us to be patient, and we should always remember to bear with one another in love. Make every effort to keep the unity of The Spirit through the bond of peace.

The life verses mentioned above are obviously great reminders for any marriage. If a husband and wife are humble, gentle, patient, selfless, and eager to keep the peace in their relationship, there would be a lot less fighting and hurt feelings. This verse reminds us to remain calm and do as our Lord and Savior, Yashaya Christ, would do. Please let these words sink deep into your heart and live it out in your marriage.

## Obey the Rules When Having an Argument

When you are in a relationship and you end up disagreeing or arguing, always strive to continue the discourse respectfully. Own your words because what you say to each other matters a lot. Don't offend each other on purpose or use harsh language just because you're angry and frustrated.

Usually, when people argue and say nasty, vile things to their spouse, it's what we call "verbal fists." It is like punching each other with harsh, piercing words.

When you engage in verbal assaults, it creates deep emotional wounds that can take ages to heal because of the mental scarring that it causes. Some would even say emotional abuse is worse than physical assault!

Remember, your words can be like daggers to your spouse. They can cut right to the heart and wound it beyond repair. Wherefore, set rules when you have arguments or disagreements. Always have certain boundaries that you cannot cross, no matter how intense or heated things get.

Coming together to set rules about what you will absolutely NOT say to each other, no matter how angry you get, creates a safe space to hold disagreements. It shows love and respect to your spouse, even when you aren't too happy with them. The fact that you both didn't cross over into the danger zone by breaking the rules shows that no matter what argument you have, you both still love and respect each other enough to not create emotional wounds.

The rule of thumb is to never say anything so extreme in anger that you can't recover from it through an apology.

For example, refrain from saying things like, "God, I wish I never married you!" or, "I hate you!" because these are extreme words that will leave your spouse scarred.

Even once you've cooled down and apologized, the emotionally injured spouse will still hold those damaging statements to heart. It is best to get rid of those weapons of mass destruction so that you can move forward and not be stuck in the past hurts of the relationship.

One of the beautiful things The Most High God has given us is the power of choice. We should always choose to divorce negative thinking and self-doubts. Instead, try to adopt a new mindset that would say, "I can do all things through Christ who strengthens me."

Our words are very powerful, so they should be used carefully and skillfully when we speak to others. There is a process that starts as we speak. We plant seeds that eventually form our persona in the mind of the other person.

In order to plant a seed in the ground, we must first cut or till the ground and then sow the seed. When we take these lessons and apply them to our life, we can say we are planting verbal seeds into our spouses, children, and anyone else that we engage with.

Therefore, it is necessary to recognize what type of seeds you are planting. Are they negative or positive? Another thing to keep in mind is that our words will come back to us in one form or another, much like the seeds producing a harvest in your garden. Wherefore, based on whatever you plant, be ready to deal with the harvest accordingly. Life and death lie in the power of the tongue.

Research studies suggest that when we speak words, there is a biological response that causes hormones to be released. When we speak negative words, we release negative energy and thereby planting negative seeds into our spouse's emotional soil.

When these verbal seeds are planted, they cause a release of negative chemicals resulting in anxiety, stress, tension, anger, and physical sickness. Your spouse internalizes the words that you say, even if they don't show it.

Think about this for a moment. If your spouse already suffers from low self-esteem, feelings of worthlessness, and past hurt, belittling them through harsh and reckless words would only worsen their mental trauma. You are supporting the negative self-talk that they already struggle with instead of offering them motivation, love, and admiration.

The things you say will ultimately add to and become a part of their self-talk. They become the diet that they are constantly ingesting, thus causing their brains to become wired to poor self-esteem and hating who they are. What a horrible thing to put your spouse through!

One might say that all the spouse needs to do ignore these words or maybe even walk away from the person saying them. Yes, this is an option. But why would you risk causing such mental struggle to a person you love? You shouldn't do anything to hurt them purposefully, of course!

Furthermore, we all know some people who practice using venomous speech. These people make it their mission to verbally hurt you for no apparent reason. They take the safety off their verbal gun and fire all types of hurtful, nasty rounds at you.

Is this really the proper way to discourse? Absolutely not!

The Bible states that we should let the law of kindness rest in our mouths. Take thought that sweet (fresh) and bitter (salt) water can't flow at the same time. Thus, this type of horrible speech can never cause healthy growth in any person.

We must learn to temper our tongues and know that we can't say whatever we want to because we think it's right. There are rules to what I call "spirited debates" or arguing as well.

The words that we hear on a daily basis affect our minds and play a significant role in shaping who we are. When considering this, we must be careful about what we say for our words will be justified or condemned.

However, if you don't want issues or problems in your relationship and you are guilty of verbal fisting with your words, try to change your speech immediately.

I have heard people say that they simply want peace. However, they do not realize that they are the ones disturbing the peace in their home through harsh words and actions.

Remember that harvest time is coming, and our words will return to either punch and shoot us or edify and encourage us.

The words that return to you; Will they bear fruit or poison? At this point, your words have probably taken shape, and you are seeing the results of what you have been saying.

Have you been using your words negatively? How powerful would a couple be if they used their words to build each other up instead of tearing one another down? How much confidence would our loved ones gain if we solely spoke life to them?

The benefits of positive words far outweigh the risks.

What risk?

The risk of being humble and not letting pride dictate your words. We could begin to see life in a whole new light. It wouldn't matter how big the task; We would have enough belief in ourselves that we could speak to that mountain and make our way passed it.

Conversely, we would not have the feeling of being defeated, and we could silence those limiting beliefs that we once carried within ourselves.

Growing up, I would hear the words, "Oh, she is so strong," or, "She got this," and even, "She doesn't need anybody."

Personally, I had to break up and unearth that thought process in my life, especially after getting married. Sure, there are times when you must carry your own self-confidence. Though, once I was married, there was no way I could have held on to this mindset and still had a successful marriage.

Ladies, this type of thinking in your marriage opens a gateway for pride to enter and even destroy your marriage. That's because it stops you from honoring your husbands.

I know you probably think that it is not that deep. Oh, but it is that deep!

I have seen this type of thinking so many times. We need to realize that pride has no place in a marriage. You can be proud **OF** your marriage, but you can't have pride **IN** the marriage.

Being deeply loved by someone gives you strength, while loving someone deeply gives you courage.

~ **Lao Tzu**

# Chapter 5 - Preventing Infidelity

## *More From Tierre Berger*

Is it possible to recover from infidelity? Nothing is ever a guarantee, of course. However, you can always safeguard your relationship and give it the respect it deserves by preventing the possibility of infidelity from occurring in the first place. This will work in your favor, as well as your relationships.

There is a lot to unpack when it comes to infidelity, so let's get started.

First, you should start by establishing certain boundaries for yourself. Learn to put safeguards around you, so you won't be tempted to cross the line with the other sex.

Next, try to remember the words "pay attention to paying attention." This means that you should pay attention to yourself by taking purposeful notice of the direction of your thoughts and actions. Think of how far you are going with friends or colleagues of the opposite sex.

Are you fantasizing about a certain person? Are you being flirtatious with them? Are you presenting yourself in a sexually suggestive manner to anybody besides your partner? Are you married yet conducting yourself as if you were single?

All of these are thoughts and behaviors that you need to constantly pay attention to. You will often hear people say that there is nothing wrong with a little "harmless flirting".

Well, flirting with others while you are committed to somebody is never harmless; Let's first establish this as a fact. It is important to realize that that is everything but harmless. It can cause major disruption and hurt in your relationship.

I like to view this behavior as a gateway or a door leading straight to infidelity. Most flirting starts with general compliments, smiles, and side conversations. While the act is usually very subtle and outside the bedroom, it can lead to secrets and eventually head into the bedroom.

Let's look at a simple scenario regarding flirting. Suppose you are at a social gathering, and you repeatedly offer compliments to the same individual of the opposite sex.

For women, it may involve laughing at everything the man says, using their eyes to lure him in, and fawning over his looks, body, how well he's dressed, his cologne, his hairstyle, etc.

For men, along with compliments, it may have a more tangible presentation. Men are prone to doing things like opening the door for other women, helping them put on their coats, and assisting them by offering their hand as they step down a few steps, despite not doing any of those things for their own wives.

A good indicator to know if you are being flirtatious is noticing when you are going out of your way to gain the attention of the person or persons you are trying to impress. You may do this by saying and doing extra things that you usually wouldn't do for others.

It also includes complimenting things that only a person who was paying extra close attention would notice. An example can be complimenting the way a woman flips her hair while talking or mentioning how nice her dimples look as she smiles.

*Ecclesiasticus 27:3 (Apocrypha) says,*

"Unless a man holds himself diligently in the fear of the Lord, his house shall soon be overthrown."

This phrase is directly talking about making yourself accountable and taking notice of how you conduct yourself in every area before you fall into ruin.

Another surefire way to know if you are being flirtatious is by accepting it when your spouse says you are. Your spouse is likely to instantly notice if you are behaving differently or paying close attention to someone else, even if you don't realize it. This is especially true if you haven't been giving your spouse the same level of attention.

If your spouse comes to you with such concerns, listen to them and try to be honest with yourself. Instead of getting defensive and downplaying your actions, attempt to see things from your partner's perspective. Be honest and truthful with yourself regarding your actions.

The offender may try to justify their actions by saying things like "You are tripping," "You are acting jealous," or even "That's just my personality." They might even defend themselves by saying that they are just nice, friendly people.

These are all excuses that are said to throw you off the trail with regard to the flirtation that they are participating in. The fact is that they probably were the ones who opened the door to such conduct.

Do a self-check and be sure to consider if you are being overly complimentary, suggestive, or touchy-feely with somebody aside from your spouse. Do you behave as though you are attracted to someone or trying to attract them?

Enticing someone physically or with words indicates intentions of deception, which eventually leads to infidelity. While you may be thinking that these types of compliments are harmless, the person you are complementing might be starving for the kind of attention that you are offering. They will internalize your kind words and gestures and treat them as indications that you are interested in them.

Therefore, these people may begin to take on the idea that you are willing to take things further. The flirting exchange starts and quickly gets out of hand. You will know that this is in full effect when the person on the receiving end starts to find things to compliment you, as well.

Again, if you are going out of your way to gain the attention of anybody but your partner and if you are trying to impress them by saying and doing extra things, that classifies as flirting.

Let's say you have been married for a while, and your relationship has settled into the same old norms. You might even be finding yourself in the midst of a rut, and therefore, you are looking for some excitement in your life.

You probably wish to experience that same feeling you felt when you first met your spouse. Your quest for this feeling has you engaging in playful flirting with other people, thus creating a doorway for infidelity to enter your marriage.

Being curious about another person's life can take a life of its own. If you are sincerely not trying to be deceptive in your conversations or compliments, then it is worthwhile to change how you approach people of the other sex.

Your tone, your body language, and mannerisms will all have to change to prevent any flirtatious encounters. Make these changes with the intention of being more respectful of your relationship and your spouse.

Taking these small steps can prepare you for long-term behavior change. If the thought of complimenting someone of the opposite sex or gaining their attention does come to mind, you should remind yourself that this person is not YOUR spouse. Deny the urge to reach out to them and keep standing strong until the desire leaves for good.

You can also try to imagine that your spouse is standing directly behind you while you are flirting. Would you still behave in that manner? You most certainly would not.

*1st Corinthians 10:13*

"There hath no temptation taken you but such as is common to man: but God is faithful, who will not suffer you to be tempted above that ye are able; but will with the temptation also make a way to escape, that ye may be able to bear it."

It is understandable that you won't feel good as you work on denying the temptation. It might even appear like a missed opportunity. But that missed opportunity is your way of escaping and staying faithful to your spouse. You are going in the right direction when you avoid the opportunities to sin.

Most flirtatious behavior stems from a person wanting to see if they "still got it." Sometimes, it is merely for amusement and to have something to do, instead of serious intentions to cheat.

On the other hand, the intentions may also seem real, and people would want to explore those intentions. The problem with both scenarios emanates from a committed person's own involvement in them.

It is pertinent that you do not allow curiosity to get the better of you. The person you are flirting with has real feelings and intentions of their own, and you may not like where it goes if the flirting continues.

No one is perfect, and you might have made some missteps along the way. However, if you ever miss a shot at doing the right thing or end up giving somebody the wrong impression, do not stick to that bad habit or give up on setting it straight. As a partner, you should always strive to correct yourself.

Simply reset and improve the next time such an incident occurs. Choose not to engage in any flirtatious actions, and remember that the goal is growth, not perfection.

## Building Parameters Around Your Relationship

A good safeguard or parameter builder is including your spouse in the conversations that you have with members of the opposite sex. Whether you are interacting one-on-one or are in the company of many, speaking positively of your spouse gives the listener a mental picture of how good and well-connected your relationship is.

Involving them in the conversation is a great deterrent to things going sideways later. Therefore, conversations with members of the opposite sex should never be made in secret. If you are having a personal conversation with a member of the opposite sex, and you don't want your spouse to know about the encounter, then you probably should not be having that encounter in the first place.

If you do engage in a conversation, be sure that your spouse is aware of it. It's not that you have to check in or report to them as a child, but simply honor and respect your spouse by involving them in all parts of your life and your interactions, particularly with the opposite gender.

Doing this exposes the conversation and builds trust. Your spouse can rest assured that you are not being deceptive because they already know what's going on and can see that you have nothing to hide.

You should also examine the way you offer compliments to the opposite gender. Ask yourself if it can be interpreted as flirting.

The compliments you give may seem innocent, but are they really? An appropriate way to compliment someone will be to praise their connection to their spouse if they are married or in a relationship. This way, you can ensure that there are no negative intentions or misunderstandings from any side.

If you are on the fence about whether your compliment might be taken the wrong way, be safe and just don't say anything. It is not your responsibility to stroke their ego anyway. The notion of flirting stops being an issue when you speak highly of your spouse to the opposite sex and reserve your compliments just for them.

Although, it is not an all-out guarantee that eliminates all chances of infidelity, it can ensure that there is minimal room for wrong interpretations.

There is also another question that many people ask.

"Why do people cheat instead of walking away from the relationship?"

This is an age-old question that often leaves people perplexed. There was a study done on alcoholism, in which Alcoholics Anonymous or AA used an acronym H.A.L.T. (B). H- hungry, A-angry, L-lonely, T- Tired. It was used to identify where they were in their addiction. Many people added in B, as they were merely bored.

This was an indication that people who struggle with alcohol addiction could fall into relapse should they experience any of these feelings. Strange as it may sound, we can apply this same concept to understand why people step outside of their relationship and end up committing adultery within their marriage.

Let's take a closer look at the H.A.L.T. (B) model. We can use the same acronyms to identify the levels of contention that cause infidelity.

**H**-Hungry, shows people being hungry for more in their relationship or starving for attention from their spouse.

**A**- Angry, people who are emotionally irritated, constantly arguing with their partners, or angry about being in a rut. Many of these people may feel like their life is centered around work, home, and chores, so they need some mental stimulation and purpose.

**L**-Lonely, people often feel lonely, despite having a partner and children. This could be because they feel like they are not being seen or aren't appreciated and valued as they deserve.

**T**- Tired, people can easily get tired of the same routine. Tired and emotionally fatigued people often look for a jolt of energy or a spark of exhilaration.

We are adding B also, as it does cause infidelity.

**B**-Bored, feelings of boredom are emphasized when we feel stuck in a situation and find ourselves looking for something exciting to stimulate us.

You may have heard the saying, "an idle mind is the devil's playground." It applies perfectly here, as a state of boredom causes us to waste time, overeat, and get sucked into addictions. It also causes us to neglect important social skills.

These same attributes can cause people to become unfaithful in their marriages. If you find yourself having one or all these feelings, you can combat them by getting curious about your own partner all over again. Focus on getting to know them from the beginning and asking what, if anything, they may want or need from you emotionally, physically, or spiritually. This often opens the doorway for you to then express your wants and needs as well. The key is having constant open communication with your spouse.

A great many people forget that while they are busy chasing after other people, they are putting themselves in danger of losing what they have at home.

Remember that the grass is greener where it is watered the most, albeit across the street or even in your own yard. Water your own yard because once that is gone, you may spend a lifetime trying to find a replacement but still never find it.

It is then that you realize that you already had everything, and you let it slip right out of your fingers like it was nothing. Don't be the person that drops a diamond trying to pick up rocks. They're both stones, but one holds value while the other is dead weight.

# How to Move Past Infidelity

In order to move forward in your relationship and get past the infidelity, the person who cheated will need to reveal the truth and admit it to their partner.

When infidelity happens, it can feel as if your world is torn apart, and your relationship will never recover, and rightfully so. Cheating is a massive betrayal of trust, and it can be difficult to rebuild a sense of security once you've gone behind each other's back. Nevertheless, despite the betrayal and pain, there are still ways to recover if both partners are willing to put in the work. If you both have a desire to continue the relationship but don't quite know how to take things forward, aim to follow these steps.

## #1 Confession

If infidelity happens in your marriage and you both choose to work through it, the first thing that needs to take place is a sincere apology.

The offender needs to take one hundred percent of the responsibility for the infidelity. Don't blame your indiscretion on anything that your spouse did or did not. Do not mention the reasons behind why it happened or give excuses. You chose to do it, and no matter what led to the infidelity, you still made a conscious decision to cheat.

It was your responsibility to make the right decision and not get involved with somebody else, yet, you did it anyway!

Next, the affair needs to be ended completely. Close that door, lock it shut and throw away the key. One may say that is easier said than done because now you have feelings for the other person and do not want to hurt them. However, you need to know that problems will continue to reoccur if you don't let go of your infidelity completely.

Most people leave the door to their infidelity seemingly closed, but if left even slightly open, this tiny space will offer an opportunity for the offense to happen again, and it most likely will.

While your concern for the other person may be genuine, you are forgetting that you're causing pain to the person with whom you have made a covenant before God.

In conclusion, make the decision to shut the door completely and put this safety measure in place to assure your spouse that you want to stay and fight for your marriage. Prove to them that you are going to work harder to rebuild from your mistake because you think your relationship is worth it.

## #2 Forgiveness

Forgiveness is something thrown around quite effortlessly and loosely by everyone nowadays. People are quick to say, "You're supposed to forgive!" While this may be true, I wonder if we really understand how powerful forgiveness is, why it's necessary, and what it truly does.

After a murder conviction, the offender may ask for a level of forgiveness. If someone gets caught stealing, they may ask for forgiveness in hopes of suffering from less severe consequences.

*Matthew 6:14-15 NIV*

14 For if you forgive other people when they sin against you, your heavenly Father will also forgive you.

15 But if you do not forgive others their sins, your Father will not forgive your sins.

Forgiveness means you accept what wrongs have been done to you, and you choose to let go of those wrongs. You work on calming your heart with God's love and patience, and you begin again with that person as forgiveness frees you to continue together.

On the other hand, even if you decide that you can't stay married to somebody who has betrayed you, forgiveness is still essential to your growth. It will help you move on without them in your life and help you form better, healthier relationships without past trauma weighing you down.

Forgiveness doesn't mean you continue to engage with people who have proven their disloyalty, time and time again. It just means that you rise above their actions and let go of them, so they don't wear you down. Once you have forgiven, the choice is yours whether to stay or go because you are free of this emotional baggage either way.

Forgiveness after infidelity can be a difficult thing to achieve. We often say I can forgive, but I will "never forget." The good news is you don't have to.

To be honest, we really are not supposed to forget, as the lesson that we have learned is there to keep us safe. However, forgiving but not forgetting does mean that you don't use the incident as a weapon to emotionally beat up your partner and rehash it at will.

Forgiveness is so crucial, as it is for your benefit and not the offender's. You can forgive and still have emotions about it. Forgiveness is a process, and it will be your journey to go on.

One might wonder, "How can I do that when I don't feel like forgiving that person?" We must remember that Christ forgave our sins, and we are to follow his example. Society has taught us to live in our feelings, but numerous studies have proven that doing so is directly linked to sickness. The stress of not forgiving weighs you down and can harm you physically, mentally, and emotionally.

It can raise your cortisol levels which in turn can cause digestive issues and even lead to alterations in your immune system.

For this reason, the best thing you can do for yourself is to let go of the anger and the decision not to forgive. This will help you heal your mind, spirit, and body.

Following what society has taught us, i.e., to live in our feelings, leads you to the pathway of emotional and physical illnesses.

Instead, you should know that forgiveness is not a feeling; it is a decision you actively make. If you are looking for a feeling of being forgiving, the chances are that it will never come after what your partner has put you through.

However, you can make the decision to offer your forgiveness and see how your feelings begin to change.

Now for the offenders. If your partner has given you the gift of forgiveness, this is not to be taken lightly. It is now your job to cherish this gift and do everything you possibly can to show them that you have learned your lesson. Give them confidence that you won't ever repeat the dreadful mistake you made and express your shame in having done so.

If you have been cheated on, you might find yourself wondering, "How long will it take me to get over this and forgive?" That, my friend, is a difficult question to answer as your trauma is your personal experience. No one can tell you how long to live in it or what exactly you should do to get out of it, as it varies from person to person.

However, what I can tell you is that the sooner you make the decision to stop being angry and reluctant to forgive, the sooner you will begin to heal.

Remember that you are human too and prone to making mistakes yourself. Perhaps one day, you may find yourself asking for forgiveness as well. You know you would want to be forgiven and for people to recognize the efforts you have made to rectify the incident. Endeavour to do the same yourself.

Forgiveness is a process, and there may still be emotions and feelings tied to your trauma. In spite of this, you should know that it is okay to feel how you feel. This is your journey, and you can take things one day at a time until you're fully ready to move on from the infidelity.

Also, let me assure you that forgiveness doesn't mean you are endorsing the behavior of your spouse. It just means that you are making yourself free from the bondage and entanglement that comes with having the spirit of not forgiving.

Offering forgiveness is an opportunity to set new boundaries and perimeters regarding your relationship. It is now the offender's job to start a journey of healing and recovery with you. They should be showing empathy and patience every step of the way.

It is such a beautiful thing to know Christ as he gave us the gift of forgiveness through his blood, even though we didn't deserve it.

Giving forgiveness is a matter of the heart, a gift you give to others to free yourself. If you find that you are unable to forgive, we encourage you to think about the sacrifice that Christ gave for us. In choosing to stay in the marriage, you absolutely need to forgive.

### #3 Counseling / Coaching

If you have made the decision to stay in your marriage, it is important that you get external help through marital counseling or coaching. Doing this shows your spouse that you are willing to put in the work to heal together and get your relationship back on track.

Through counseling, you will be able to identify the root causes of the problems in your relationship and see what opened the door for the infidelity to occur.

What did your partner need that they ended up seeking intimacy outside of your relationship?

As a specialized component of life coaching, relationship coaching helps people find greater fulfillment in their partnerships. These are all things that can be discovered through marital coaching.

Let us look at the differences between Marital Counseling and Marriage Coaching.

In many situations, couples in a marriage can get confused about what kind of help they want or need. If you are searching for help in a marriage, here is some insight to help you better understand whether you require marriage counseling or marriage coaching to fix your relationship.

Marriage Counseling:

Marriage counseling is often more formal, more intensive, and more clinical. Marriage counselors have formal education and experience in relevant topics such as psychology, social work, etc.

Counseling occurs in a formal office and has a regular meeting schedule. It is often seen as a more extreme treatment for a marriage because it deals with mending relationships after a significant negative event or occurrence.

Since counselors have formal education and certification, they can treat problems around mental health and provide clinical solutions to the problems at hand.

Marriage Coaching:

This process is more casual and personalized. Marriage coaches often rely on their years of personal experience and may or may not have formal education in the subject. Coaching is personal regarding flexibility in meeting times as the coach focuses more on you and your spouse's relationship.

Instead of meeting in a formal office, coaches can meet in houses, coffee shops, online, etc. They make a strong effort to get to know you personally instead of labeling you into a specific group.

Both counselors and coaches are highly valuable and, depending on the specific need of the relationship, can help you make your way back to each other in your relationship.

Some couples may feel like they need to get professional help from a full-time counselor, while others may need the laid-back approach of coaching.

## #4 Put the Most High God Back into Your Marriage

The Bible is the blueprint through which all successful marriages thrive. The holy scriptures teach us how to conduct ourselves in various situations, especially in a marital relationship.

We sometimes tend to forget that marriage is God's institution, and therefore, He must be in the center of it. When we get married, we form a covenant with our spouse in the sight of The Most High by repeating these words.

"I ___take you___ to be my lawfully wedded wife or husband. To have and to hold from this day forward, for better or for worse, for richer or for poorer, in sickness and in health, to love and to cherish, till death we do us part. According to God's holy ordinance, this is my solemn vow."

Once we get married, we forget to follow the scriptures concerning marriage. We tend to want to do things our way and according to how we feel rather than what the scriptures direct. This is where we mess things up because we are making decisions based on our feelings instead of through God's teachings. It is important to let go of your emotions and abide by the wisdom and rationale of the scriptures.

*Hebrews 13:4 KJV*

"Marriage is honorable in all, and the bed undefiled: but whoremongers and adulterers God will judge."

This is where Satan plays a dirty game on us. He knows The Most High must judge sin, as a result his goal is to encourage us to sin so that we will be judged.

In *Exodus 20:3-17 KJV Verse 14* says,

"Thou shall not commit adultery."

When a person falls into adultery, it must be judged. By breaking the covenant made between ourselves, our spouse, and God through adultery, we thereby transgress and break the law of The Most High God, which is therefore sin.

*1 John 3:4 KJV*

"Whosoever committeth sin transgresseth also the law: for sin is the transgression of the law."

Does knowing the laws of The Most High God save you from damnation? No, Christ saves us from that, and he alone can keep us from the fire.

Does following the laws of The Most High God keep you safe? Yes, absolutely!

By putting The Most High God back into your relationship, you can ensure that both you and your spouse stay on track and live out your lives the correct way.

*Revelation 2:4 DLNT*

"But I have this against you, that you have left your first love."

Get back to trusting and believing that The Most High can restore your life, your relationships, and your purpose.

*John 15:16 NASB*

"You did not choose Me, but I chose you, and appointed you that you would go and bear fruit, and that your fruit would remain. (Your deeds, actions, and results remain.) so that whatever you ask of the Father in my name He may give to you."

In order to move forward in your relationship and get past the infidelity, you will have to work on all the steps mentioned above. Only then can you begin to foster openness and honesty. It will resonate deeply in your relationship and allow you to feel understood and heard again.

When you follow all these steps, you create a higher probability of faithfulness and happiness going forward opposed to letting your relationship become one that is wandering or drifting.

Remember to take ownership of your actions, whether they are good or bad. Take responsibility, OWN IT, and move further with your spouse!

What we have once enjoyed we can never lose. All that we love deeply becomes a part of us.

~ Helen Keller

# Chapter 6 - Developing a New You

The recovery of any damaged relationship can seem like a long and daunting road to getting back what was lost. However, applying the new "tools" you may have discovered in this book, along with the practice of patience, can definitely get you there.

We often forget how important patience really is. In fact, amid a society where we want everything in a hurry, patience is truly a lost skill! In our modern world, if you can get it, do it, or see it first, you are declared a winner. Yet, scriptures place heavy importance on being patient. This week, investigate and take notice of the level of patience you have towards your spouse or fiancée.

*James 1:4 KJV*

(4) "But let patience have her perfect work, that ye may be perfect and entire, wanting nothing."

*Ephesians 4:2-6 KJV*

(2) "With all lowliness and meekness, with long suffering, forbearing one another in love; (3) Endeavoring to keep the unity of the Spirit in the bond of peace. (4) There is one body, and one Spirit, even as ye are called in one hope of your calling: (5) One Lord, one faith, one baptism, (6) One God and Father of all, who is above all, and through all, and in you all."

We are being called to become single (one). This refers to singleness in purpose, singleness in our worship of The Most High, not idols, and singleness in the attention we give our spouse. This passage of scripture in Ephesians 4:4-6 uses the word "one" quite often. It goes to the reason why we, being many, are called to become one body. If that is the case, then we need to view our spouse as ourselves and be completely humble and gentle. We must be patient and forbear one another in love. Make every effort to keep the unity of the Spirit through the bond of peace.

This life verse is surely a great reminder for marriages, as well as relationships in general. If a husband and wife are humble, gentle, selfless, patient, and eager to keep the peace in their relationship, then there will be a lot less fighting and hurt feelings. The same holds true in any relationship. This verse also reminds us to remain calm and do as Christ Yashaya would do.

In like manner, don't expect to be perfect, be patient. The word-perfect means:

(a) being complete in all its parts

(b) full-grown, of full age

(c) the completeness of high moral character

In other words, it is a state of being mature. Displaying patience is a part of being mature, as you can't become mature without the process of developing into maturity. You were not fully grown at birth; instead, you had to go through developmental stages. It was a journey.

The CDC has what is called a "Developmental Milestones Chart," where children from 2 months to 5 years of age are categorized under different developmental stages. Skills such as taking the first step, smiling for the first time, waving bye, crawling, walking, etc., are all included in this. In time, children reach additional milestones as they age in how they play, learn, speak, act, and move on their way to becoming an adult.

Once you become an adult, you understand that life is a process. Having maturity gives you a level of confidence in knowing that you have been in similar situations before, and this helps you stay calm and not stress out or panic.

You've faced failure before, and it did not kill you. What doesn't kill you only makes you stronger if you have learned a lesson from it.

Moving towards success means going through poor attempts too. What may look like a bad attempt at practicing actually allows you to get better at your craft or pursuits later. For example, it may seem hard to implement the tools you have just acquired in this book at first but keep trying and practice!

In your determination to keep going, your viewpoint will surely change. You will stop seeing the things you attempt as losses but rather as lessons that allow you to experience a different perspective of what did not work. Embrace your unique experiences and grow from them.

Here are a few good behaviors that will help you transform into a better "you":

# #1. Don't be a Petty Person

Petty people are always fighting and arguing over things that have little to no importance. Maybe you know some people who seem to be petty about everything all the time. We are all guilty of having petty thoughts sometimes that may need to be worked on. It doesn't automatically mean that you are toxic or abusive.

However, it can be part of a much wider pattern of abusive behavior. Pettiness can be used to manipulate people and situations. It is the quality or condition of being unkind, stingy, or ungenerous, especially in small or minor things. Pettiness can be very mean-spirited, which is one reason why we shouldn't normalize it.

# #2. Don't Major in the Minors

The size of the problems and issues that you focus on symbolizes the size of who you are mentally. Small-minded people focus on problems and complain about every insignificant little issue, just like a petty person.

For women, it may look like being upset at your husband and wanting to call it quits merely because he doesn't rub your feet, or he doesn't know how you feel at the very moment. You might be ignoring all the wonderful things he does for you, like providing for the home, loving you, caring for you and the children, etc. But, because he didn't rub your feet, you placed all your focus there.

For men, if you are hungry and tired, then every word that comes out of your spouse's mouth feels annoying. If you're full and rested, you are happy to listen. Remember that your feelings will lie to you and tell you things that may not be valid. Feelings will cause you to disregard rationale and what is true for false expectations. Sometimes we can confuse our feelings with the will of The Most High, but there are a few Bible scriptures that can help one separate between spirit and soul.

_Hebrews 4:12_ (KJV) says it best:

"For **the word of God** is quick, and powerful, and sharper than any two-edged sword, piercing even to the dividing asunder of soul and spirit, and of the joints and marrow, and is a discerner of the thoughts and intents of the heart."

This scripture shows us that the word of God shines its penetrating light upon the inner man. Faithfulness begins with a proper internal gauge. The quick and powerful word of The Most High probes into the deepest part of a person like a surgeon's knife to discern its innermost thoughts and intents. God's word reveals to him both his ingrained wickedness and the saving way of faith at that critical point. When the divine judge reveals himself through his word, the hearer must labor to enter the divine rest by believing. We can never be led by the Holy Spirit until we allow ourselves to be led by God's word.

*Acts 2:38 KJV*

"Then Peter said unto them, Repent and be baptized every one of you in the name of Yashaya (Hebrew) Christ for the remission of sins, and you shall receive the gift of the Holy Spirit."

The gift of the Holy Spirit lives in our spirit once we are baptized. When we get confused trying to decide what we should do in any situation, we always look to God's word for the correct guidance. If that feeling or desire you have does not agree with the Word, then it is wrong. You cannot live by the "If something feels good, go for it" or "If something feels wrong, don't do it" mentality.

Allowing our feelings to be our guide because we can feel good about the wrong thing, like stealing or committing adultery, is a very dangerous game to play. People can build cases defending why they did what they did and make it sound legitimate. For example, someone saying they stole something because they needed it more than the person who owned it. Or, in an adulterous affair, it may sound like, "My spouse never pays me any attention anyway; They don't know me." Or "I haven't been happy in a long time; I needed something for me."

Sounding genuine to make a case for allowing your feelings to be your guide is foolish. It's amazing how, when people are caught stealing, cheating, or anything else, those feelings they once had change like the wind. Every day we live, we have a choice and a chance.

Remember, you can't wish your way out of something you behaved your way into. You must change your behavior(s).

What may help tremendously is to remember that you didn't get into your situation or condition overnight, so it may take a little time and patience to fix or reset your set of circumstances. One issue at a time, one day at a time. True fulfillment comes from knowing what your purpose is and settling into your life's work.

It's not enough to work or want to be successful just so you can be rich and show off your wealth. The one who thinks of him or herself as superior to all always cares about him or herself only. They have no time for other people, no feelings for other people, and no mindset of lifting others.

Think about yourself; Do you buy expensive gadgets, cars, or clothes? Whose money are you spending? All yours. You're hitting your own pocket. You'd never get something phenomenal in return. There are only three reasons behind every show:

1.  **We do it to build or maintain our value.**

2.  **We do it to protect our identity.**

3.  **We do it to make other people feel jealous.**

There's nothing wrong with the first two reasons if we're doing it for your goodwill. The sole reason behind showing off value and identity is to present ourselves in our best possible version. If you're doing it to poke someone or give them a feeling of disgust where they think they're worthless, then you should stop. Showing off and bragging are signs of immaturity and delayed development, and you will not be fulfilled by it in the long run.

## #3. Do Not Harbor Hatred and Unforgiveness

Unforgiveness and hatred will stunt your growth in the same way that showing off, and bragging does. Your emotional, mental, and spiritual development will suffer along the way to your destination. As a part of my mature walk, I live by an empowering profound statement that my mother once spoke to me concerning unforgiveness.

She said, "Unforgiveness is the equivalent of you drinking the poison and expecting it to kill the person that offended you."

Do not allow the poison of not forgiving to rob you of your health and liberty. Once again, she was right. Once again, forgiveness does not mean you continue to engage with people who have demonstrated their disloyalty, over and over again. On the contrary, it makes you free to do so, should you choose to. You are not tied to the hurt of that disappointment any longer, and your growth towards maturity can continue because now, you are equipped with an understanding of how to navigate and deal with various types of people that present themselves to you. This experience gives you wisdom and maturity.

## #4. Feed What You Want to Live in Your Marriage and Starve What You Want to Die Out of Your Marriage

Again, I must reiterate the importance of remembering to keep love growing by expressing love for one another, or it will die, and you will drift apart. Love and happiness are not found by seeking them for yourself but rather by giving them to each other. Whatever you are doing that does not yield the desired result means you are feeding it and, thereby, causing it to become stronger to produce more of the same.

You starve that out by doing the opposite of what you have done to cause the negative result(s).

If saying "I love you" has been a rarity in your relationship, then feeding your relationship with more words of affection will strengthen the bond between you two.

Did you know that you teach people how to treat you by what you allow or put up with? You teach people how to treat you every day. You are the teacher, and the people you encounter daily are the students. If you expect loyalty and honesty, but you accept someone who lies and cheats on you, you are teaching them that this is okay to continue.

If you expect communication, but you continuously accept people in your life who do not communicate, then you are teaching them that it is okay not to talk. When you show respect for others as well as for yourself, you only deal with people who can match your treatment by being respectful of who you are and what you deserve.

This is a big aspect of self-love. When you love yourself, you will not accept a meal of poor treatment from people in your life. When you love yourself, you will set boundaries that people will understand and respect.

Taking a step back, it is essential to understand that you cannot teach people how to treat you if you are not clear about what you want and, more importantly, what you need. Wants are things that you would like in your life but are not essential. Needs, on the other hand, are things that you must have in your life in order to be truly happy—to truly make you feel good.

When we think of the idea of developing a new you, not only is it necessary, but it is something you will be doing for the rest of your life. Let's look at an analogy that I am sure all of us can relate to in some way.

In the world of technology, we receive a message on a computer that says, "New software update available would you like to install it now?" Many of us dismiss this message for numerous reasons. However, if we continue to ignore this message, our computers will eventually start slowing down and become vulnerable to viruses and bugs simply due to our refusal to make the necessary changes and keep our computers updated.

Now, let's look at this same scenario in a different way. This time, you are receiving a new message for your life, and it says, "New tools available, would you like to try them now?" What if we did the same with this new information we've gotten and ignored it? One day, we will subject ourselves to the viruses and bugs of life.

365 days from today, if you haven't downloaded any of the new information and tried applying what you have received into your life, the viruses of laziness, not knowing what to do, and staying

stuck will rob you of your purpose and happiness. To remedy the possibility of these things happening, is to agree to the terms and update our life's software. These updates will allow you to quickly navigate all of life's challenges, tests, and trials.

However, the download is only activated by faith in action. Faith is believing that you can be better and will cause you to act! Action is the key to greatness. The Bible says, "Faith is the substance of things hoped for and the evidence of things not seen." Simply put, faith is the absence of any physical evidence, but you work it into existence. We must be willing to download and go through the updates of life to make the appropriate changes.

As we allow these updates that we receive in the form of new information, techniques, and behaviors, we will be better equipped to face the challenges that life brings. The changes that we face in life prepare us for the next update in our lives.

1st *Corinthians 13:7* explains that charity (love) "Beareth all things, believeth all things, hopeth all things and endureth all things."

Love never fails! Yashaya is the epitome of love, and by using him as an example, we are capable of giving our spouse the same type of love; The type of love that bears all things, believes all things, hopes all things, and endures all things. The word endure is derived from the Greek word "Hypomeno," which means to remain and to persevere under misfortune and trials, in this case, to hold fast to one's faith in Yashaya.

Sometimes the road may be rough, and our well thought out plans blow up in our faces.

*Proverbs 19:20-21 KJV*

"Hear counsel, and receive instruction, that thou mayest be wise in thy latter end. 21 There are many devices (plans and thoughts) in a man's heart; nevertheless, the counsel of The Most High, that shall stand."

Continue to revive the courtesy of courtship in your married life. Successful marriages don't just happen; they must be developed. It is not always the big things that make a difference; remember, the little things count just as much. If we continue to remind ourselves to pay attention to the small details in our marriages, then we will find that the bigger issues are handled a lot easier.

Having faith stops you from a defeated belief that puts limits on what you can do and obtain. Start having faith that you can once again obtain a life worth living. I am not by any means suggesting that you should live without barriers and standards, for that is a form of discipline that is most necessary in our lives. You must have discipline. Discipline is having the correct parameters in your pursuits and not just doing any and everything to get ahead.

## The Secret to Gaining Traction During a Disagreement

In any relationship, you will have some disagreements. The key is not to turn it into a personal attack on your spouse. Argue with the argument, not with the person. Instead of saying *you are wrong*, say *here is my issue with that*.

When you argue in such a manner, you allow the argument to be the issue and not your spouse. If your argument requires people to dismantle their egos in order to agree with you, they are not going to agree with you. On the other hand, if you make the argument your opponent and not your spouse, they are more likely to agree and not take it personally. Since courting and marriage are very serious ventures, they must be approached with a spirit of excellence.

Immature love says: 'I love you because I need you.' Mature love says 'I need you because I love you.'

~ **Erich Fromm**

# Chapter 7 - Developing *into* the New You

As we bring this journey of relationships to a close, we hope you feel inspired and recharged to **"Do it again."** Re-start, rekindle, and renew the passion that once burned bright in your relationship as you rediscover your purpose in life and chart out the right direction to take in your relationship. Stay persistent in your pursuits. Don't give up, don't cave in, and don't quit. You can do it!

All it takes is having a purpose and acting on it to get going. However, before we part ways, we want you to consider another caveat that can hinder, prolong, or even stop your development and hold you back from accomplishing any achievements in life. The only thing that stops your forward movement is no movement at all. In other words, the main culprit is procrastination.

Procrastination has overwhelmed many when it comes to taking action in marriage, business, or any other note-worthy cause. For example, a couple may find it difficult to have meaningful conversations in their relationship about what they need. Therefore, they end up putting it off and delaying any attempts to talk it out.

According to Wikipedia, procrastination is the action of unnecessarily and voluntarily delaying or postponing something despite knowing that there will be negative consequences for it. Procrastinating behavior is often termed as a "slow pressure-cooking relationship issue" by relationship coaches. This is mainly because, and I quote, "Procrastination will gradually grow and become the main issue over your years of being together."

Putting off important conversations, or procrastinating, can have damaging and self-sabotaging side effects. Ask yourself if you are being as productive as possible in your marriage, business, or relationship pursuits. If not, then maybe you are just doing the bare minimum that you can get away with.

If the latter is true, then you might have a bad habit that needs to be fixed. Procrastinators are often considered **perfectionists** since they tend to be people who refuse to accept any standard shy of perfection. Psychologically, they believe that it is more acceptable to never tackle a job than to face the possibility of it not going well. People who procrastinate may care about what others will think of them, and because of that, they put their future endeavors at risk.

All of this is to avoid being judged negatively by others. I personally used to be the one who waited until the last minute to complete an assignment or a task, thinking that I would operate better under pressure. What I've come to realize is that most procrastinators think that they do better under pressure as well.

While they may be able to accomplish their tasks, they are actually experiencing the euphoria of beating a deadline after having procrastinated. This isn't a healthy practice, and there are certain factors that need to be addressed to change the behavior of a procrastinator.

First, you must alter the emotions that are tied to procrastination. Second, you have to learn to face the physical uneasiness and anxiety that you may be experiencing because of having a due date. Some procrastinators may feel overwhelmed about a particular task, so they deal with it by simply avoiding it. Avoidance and ease are the main enemies of positive productivity. Instead of avoiding a task, embrace it. Learn to actively engage in the task and realize the fact that adequate time and effort can be your ally rather than an enemy.

To grow, you must have patience. Remember to practice because growth happens with time and effort. Change doesn't just happen; you must put in the effort to develop into the person you want to be. Practice improving yourself by not putting things off anymore.

The Bible states:

*Proverbs 14:23 KJV*

*"In all labor there is profit: but the talk of the lips tends only to penury (poverty)."*

This means that if all you are doing is talking about doing wonderful things without literally working on making them a reality, then you will not have any progress. You must put in the effort, which is not necessarily "hard work" but the consistent and diligent effort that produces the results for progress.

Start by working on one task at a time and see it to its end. Then, you can start work on your next task. It is easy to mistake "hard work" and being busy as symbols of productivity, but don't confuse the two. You could be working hard and doing a hundred different things yet still be unproductive.

When a person realizes that everything they have been doing is unproductive, feelings of frustration can overwhelm them. Doing a bunch of things but still not getting the results you want is the equivalent of a vehicle being stuck in the mud as compared to one being on the pavement.

Of course, when you press the gas pedal in both scenarios, the tires will spin. The major difference here is that one vehicle is stuck spinning in its place while the other is getting to its destination. If the person stuck in the mud tries to mash the gas pedal harder while turning the steering wheel from left to right, they will just be wasting their energy and time without any movement forward.

In most cases, even being hyper-busy will not produce the results you want. It's ok to slow down a bit and reexamine your efforts. In slowing down, you do less, but you can improve your focus on one thing at a time and accomplish it completely.

## Prioritize and Learn to Say No

Many people suffer from the need to please everyone. They find themselves saying yes to everything so that the people around them are happy. They often end up delaying their own work and worrying later about how to manage everything that they have agreed to.

Start your day today by ignoring the need to please everyone and learn to say no! This can take some practice, so you should begin by saying no to something small, expressing your opinion about something simple, or taking a stand for something you believe in. Each step helps you gain more confidence in your ability to be yourself.

You might be wondering, why is trying to please everyone a bad habit?

Well, trying to please people can put you in a place where you don't have the capacity to take care of your own business. You will find yourself so overwhelmed with work that you can't even enjoy some leisure time for yourself because your day is filled with other people's wants and needs.

If you cannot do what is being asked of you, or even if you just do not want to participate, then let that be known. It does not have to be an ugly exchange. In fact, saying no can be liberating. If you are really struggling with letting go of your people-pleasing habits, seek professional help. A good therapist or a life coach can guide you on how to build your mental strength to build the kind of life you really want to live. **("10 Signs You're a People-Pleaser - Psychology Today")**

If you choose to do less, it means you will have to say no. People might be disappointed or even hurt about you saying no in the beginning, especially if you have always said yes, but hopefully, they will learn to respect your choices. **("The Art of Slowing Down for Hyper-busy, multi-tasking ...")**

## Put in the Work

To reap the benefits of gaining the skill and confidence that you need in any given area of weakness, you must work on what you are not good at. Proficiency is achieved through repetition and practice. You must practice doing what is uncomfortable to gain the confidence you need to move forward in life. It has been said that repetition is the mother of skill, so make repetition your friend and use your time wisely.

Do not squander time by doing nothing, sitting back, and wishing for things to be better. Instead, put in the work and effort of practical exercise and practice. The Bible states that our days are numbered **(Job 14:5).** Even if you lived to be a hundred years old, know that one day your time here will end. So, it is important to recognize this as reality and allow it to motivate you to start working on everything that you wish to accomplish.

What are you waiting for?

Your time is now!

What legacy do you want your family to inherit? Is it one of progressiveness or procrastination? The choice is yours. We all have the same 24 hours each day, which equates to 1,440 minutes. The real key to being successful is to determine what you choose to do with the time that you have. Some people use it to become better and develop the outcomes they desire, while others sit back, complain, blame, and refuse to put in the work needed to improve their situation.

You can choose to live with purpose, or you can choose to give your life over to chance. This means living with the possibility of something good happening yet refusing to put in the work required to achieve it. Either way, **time keeps on slipping into the future**.

Although everyone's situation and circumstances may be different, we are still responsible for how we organize and manage our own allotted time. Think about this; there are people in prison right now who are spending the same amount of time in jail that you are spending free in society. Hence, the problem isn't the absence of time; the problem is the quality of your time. It is about where and how you are spending your time.

In relationships, you either do time with your spouse or you thrive in time with them. Doing time is just counting the years you have been married and using that as a badge of honor. Remember that it does not mean you have a good connection or a solid relationship. Thriving in marriage means you are growing and developing in a continual, open, and honest relationship through sharing of thoughts and feelings. You share your heart and soul with your partner and develop a connection where you feel safe enough to share your joys and dreams, as well as your sorrows and fears.

This feeds the emotional connection in the relationship. Emotional intimacy helps couples thrive amidst the difficulties of life. It is true that counting the years you have been married is honorable and should be well-respected. Nevertheless, while counting the years, you should also consider the quality (how well) and the quantity (the length) of your relationship. Quality brings deeper levels of joy than the number of years you have spent together.

Do not allow your relationship to become diminished by not giving it the proper attention it needs. Love is not a sentimental impulse but a holy principle that is included in every phase and action of your life. With true love, your marriage cannot fail. **("Keys for a Happy Marriage | To Bear Witness of the Light ...")**

Without it, it cannot succeed. **(1 Cor 13:4-7)**

We often have a myriad of reasons why we don't do or practice the skill of bettering ourselves. Some people say things like, "I have kids and I have to work so I can't do ____." Others say, "I have a husband or wife holding me back from finishing _____." Many more say, "My job ties up most of my time so there isn't any time left to work on _____."

Keep in mind that all these reasons might be legitimate, but they are still dull in comparison to the dreams that we give up on by using them.

Are you taking a chance and hoping that your excuses will diminish, disappear, and make way for you to really go after what you want? The real fact of the matter is that they will not. Not now, not ever.

You must grab the steering wheel of your life purposefully and drive it where you want it to go. Tell yourself that losing is not an option for you; you absolutely cannot fail. Suppose you do try to better your relationship and make it happen! Just suppose you went ahead and started your business or pursued any other dreams, and it worked out.

What would be the impact of achieving that desire for you? What about your family? How would your lifestyle change? Would it be for the better or worse? With your desires accomplished just 365 days from today, what kind of life would you be able to enjoy? Why wait an entire year when you can achieve it **now** if you truly try to?

All you must do is believe in it, plan for it, and execute it. As you continue to read on, I want you to picture yourself accomplishing your goals. Now allow yourself, for just a moment, to feel the success. Feel the accomplishment of having a beautiful, thriving, and healthy relationship. You deserve it!

You have done the work to get to where you are.

Picture yourself on the other side of your problems and think of what that feels like. If you follow this short exercise, you will feel your emotions shift to a different place; a place where you are open to feelings of accomplishment. See, your mind cannot tell the difference between what is real and what is make-believe when it comes to your feelings. If you can feel the accomplishments and feel the health and happiness your body will shift to that kind of natural feeling, and you will start to feel good.

Congratulations! You just operated in faith.

*Hebrews 11:1* declares:

"Faith is the substance of things hoped for, the evidence of things not seen."

Unfortunately, like most individuals, we tend to concentrate more on the negative than on the positive. We tend to rely more on our own thoughts than on the word of The Most High God. When you use your time to think and ponder over positive things, that is what you will be attracted to.

Negativity is what will be drawn towards you when you use your time to think of the negatives. Your body will shift to that level of thinking as well, and you will start to feel worse. Notice that while you're doing this mental conditioning exercise, you use the same amount of time as another person who may be going through the same situation. The only difference is that they chose to worry, complain, and operate in fear instead of shifting their thoughts and aligning their actions to the word of God as you did.

The cycle of the seasons is constant. Night and day are repeated functions. Even your body itself has repeated functions. There is a time when you get sleepy and a time when you must use the restroom. These functions reoccur on time, which means you will not miss your appointment to-go. We are simply saying that your time is now, so what are you waiting for? Do not wait for things to get better before you feel good. Learn to feel good now and experience how things get better. Remember to use focused concentration because there is a distinct difference between having a vision and goals.

A vision without work and action is just a dream. Goals are an outward expression of your dreams. A goal is simply a dream with a deadline.

Let us say that you have thought of starting your own business. You should just get on with it right now. Turn your thoughts into deeds. There is no better time than the present when you can start small. If you want to start working out of your house, do that. Offer a product or service part-time you can use your evenings or your weekends; the point here is by seizing the time you have available, you will be able to start to move in the very direction that you are trying to go with precision and correctness because time is of the essence.

Get it going first; get it right later! Anything that is worth doing is worth doing badly first because as you continue forward step by step and not be distracted nor discouraged by mistakes, setbacks, or letdowns, you will learn how to do it correctly later. This is a lesson no one will ever be able to take away from you.

Sometimes in life, we can find ourselves dealing with the wrong people. We don't notice that sometimes in brokenness, we may choose broken people since we attract who we are. Now that you have grown and matured, you will no longer fit well with such people. The brokenness in you attracted something in them. Had you not been in that broken place, you would have probably chosen someone different.

Once you are out of an unhealthy relationship, you must do the work of self-reflection and take a real dive into yourself. Being true to yourself and facing your fears, feelings, insecurities, and such are important right now. By doing so, you can have a better gauge of what type of people you need in your life.

You should never be afraid to try because you will fail. Have you ever heard the statement "Fail your way to the top?" It might sound funny, but it is oh so true!

Failure is not a life sentence but a lesson. It offers lessons and learning about what not to do, how to do it better, etc. Always remember that the lesson is not failure but what you do after it.

**Men!**

Remember what we used to say to women- It costs to be the boss!

Yes! It costs to be the boss, but understand that the real fee isn't "just" financial; it's your faith. Walk with The Most High, lay your foundation in God's word, and be fervent in your prayer over her. Stay dedicated to your faithfulness to her, your friendship with her, your flowing love for her, the facts you speak, the fruit of your spirit, etc.

Most importantly, pay attention to how she feels when you're together or apart. Recognize the power in your works and your words. Every man, regardless of their career level, has access to these types of funds. No loans, background checks, or credit checks are required, just your willingness to do what's important to her and you.

**MEN** - DO YOUR RESEARCH AND INVEST WISELY.

**WOMEN** - INVEST IN YOURSELF, SO WHEN YOUR MR. RIGHT COMES; YOU KNOW HOW TO HANDLE IT.

*1 Corinthians 11:3* BSB

"But I want you to know that the head of every man is Christ, the head of woman is man, and the head of Christ is God."

Yes! It costs to be the boss. So, my question is, what type of funds do you have available for this investment?

End.

Time is too slow for those who wait, too swift for those who fear, too long for those who grieve, too short for those who rejoice, but for those who love, time is eternity.

**~ Henry Van Dyke**

# About the Authors

## Tierre Berger

Tierre Berger (MA, BA, CPC) is an Executive Coach, Mentor, Author, and Master Communicator, who is affectionately known as the Coaches' Coach. Tierre specializes in Executive Laser Coaching, which focuses on identifying root issues quickly so they can be addressed in a healthy fashion. He also does a component of youth mentoring and coaching, which helps the youth achieve clarity and direction. If you're ready to go to the next level and achieve enlightenment, I can help you improve your lifestyle and reach your desired goals.

# Jacquelyn Berger

Jacquelyn Berger (RN, BSN, BA, RC, NC) is a professional Nursing Coach, Mentor, and Author. Jacquelyn is a highly sought-after holistic Health and Wellness Nursing Coach.

In 2017, Jacquelyn was nominated and honored with the "Top 100 Nurses" award for the Dallas/Fort Worth Area. Having demonstrated superior contributions to the art and science of nursing, she upholds high standards of accountability when it comes to Health and Wellness coaching.

If you wish to work on any stagnant areas of your life and just can't seem to get it going, Nurse Coach Jacquelyn is here to lend a helping hand. Through her powerful questioning, further enhanced by her years' worth of experience as a Nurse and Life Coach, she can help you focus on any part of your life that requires a bit of polishing so you can enjoy this world to the fullest. For people who wish to get better through a holistic lifestyle approach to their health and wellness, Jacquelyn Berger really is the perfect life coach.

Jacquelyn is currently working to extend her education by becoming certified in Functional Medicine.

# Their Relationship

Tierre and Jacquelyn Berger together offer a unique approach to marital relationship coaching. This husband-and-wife power duo has shared their relationship expertise for more than 17 years to help hundreds of individuals rebuild and strengthen their marital relationships through the word of God. They realize that making God central to any relationship is essential for its success, so they promote this message to every marital union.

Equipped with keen awareness and an understanding that people who seek out relationship coaching aren't looking for a clinical diagnosis, this couple instead applies a more holistic approach to strengthening the bond of your relationship. Are you considering hiring a relationship coach to improve your marriage and base it on the grounds of trust and respect? You need Mr. and Mrs. Berger on your team to see this mission to success!

Made in the USA
Middletown, DE
08 December 2022

16409048R00073